# How to Make
# Your Car
# Last *Almost* Forever

# How to Make Your Car Last *Almost* Forever

## Jack Gillis

A PERIGEE BOOK

*For my family,*
*Marilyn, Katie and John*

Perigee Books
are published by
The Putnam Publishing Group
200 Madison Avenue
New York, NY 10016

*Designed by Rhea Braunstein*

Typeset by Fisher Composition, Inc.

Library of Congress Cataloging-in-Publication Data

Gillis, Jack.
  How to make your car last almost forever.

  1. Automobiles—Maintenance and repair—Amateurs' manuals.
I. Title.
TL152.G52  1987      629.28'722        87-14804
ISBN 0-399-51336-1

Printed in the United States of America
      4  5  6  7  8  9  10

# ACKNOWLEDGMENTS

This book would not have been possible without the invaluable assistance of two people—Karen Fierst and Teresa Talley. Karen's research skills and Teresa's magical performance on the word processor, combined with their willingness to work hard, were the primary ingredients in getting this book to print. Thanks also to Peter Zetlin for his editorial assistance and Roger Scholl for his editorial touch and overall vision of the book.

# CONTENTS

CONTENTS

CONTENTS

# INTRODUCTION

This is not a book for mechanics, car buffs, or people who want to know everything possible about how their car works and how to fix it. This is a book for those of us who have just spent a remarkable amount of money buying something that, for the most part, we know little about. Now that we have spent more than we ever thought possible on a car, we are bound and determined to keep it as long as possible.

There is really no secret to extending the life of your car. Your car should be able to provide adequate service for at least 100,000 miles. In fact, the longer you keep a car, the lower your ownership costs will be. Over time the fixed costs of a car decline. After three or four years, for example, you will have finished making your car payments, most of the depreciation will have been absorbed, and you might be able to reduce your insurance bill by trimming your coverage. Even the occasional large repair bill will be far cheaper than buying a new car. Figuring in all the costs, the Hertz Corporation determined that keeping the same car for ten rather than five years would reduce your overall expenses by at least one-third.

So how do you do it? How do you avoid all the horror stories and manage to keep a car for years? You need to do three relatively simple things: (1) develop a basic understanding of how your car works; (2) follow a regular series of preventative maintenance checks; and, (3) listen to what your car is telling you and respond with prompt repairs.

That's what this book is—a simple, straightforward guide to one of the most important and expensive products you will ever own.

How many times have you heard a strange rumble in the engine or smelled something funny? What does it really mean when one of your dash lights goes on? Knowing what a particular symptom means can be the difference between an inexpensive repair and a major overhaul. Not only is preventative maintenance fundamental to keeping your car running, but the way you drive can also affect the life of your car. In *How to Make Your Car Last Almost Forever*, I don't expect you to get on your back and adjust the clutch or get under the hood to do a tune-up. Instead, the book tells you how to check out the various components to see that they're running well and offers tips on extending their life. You'll find advice on breaking in a new car, getting through the winter, saving gas, and checking out your safety belts.

So many of us buy a new car because our present car no longer looks good. With that in mind, I've included a chapter that will tell you everything you need to know to keep that showroom sparkle, inside and out.

A few years ago a government study estimated that nearly half of every dollar spent on repairs was for either unnecessary or fraudulent work. Keeping your car for a long time inevitably means getting repairs. In this book you'll find advice on how to get the most for your repair dollar, including how to talk to a mechanic and save money in the process. You'll also learn how to get action on complaints, where you can go for help as a consumer, and how to find out if your car has been involved in a safety recall.

So why spend thousands of hard-earned dollars every couple of years on a new car when your present car can be kept running and looking like new? *How to Make Your Car Last Almost Forever* will help you get the most out of your car and help keep you out of the showroom.

# 1
## Understanding
## Your Car

## How It Works

Today's cars are so technologically sophisticated that, for most of us, their operation is a mystery. Yet, despite electronic gadgetry, computerization, and innovative aerodynamic styling, the basic operation of a car has changed little since the Model T. These next few pages will provide you with a basic understanding of how your car works and how all the systems fit together.

### Turning on the Ignition

When you turn the key to start your car, two things happen: an electric motor (the starter) cranks the engine, moving the pistons inside the cylinders, and provides electricity to the spark plugs. This is how the engine is started. How does it work? The motion of the pistons sucks a mixture of air and gasoline into the piston cylinders. The gas and air that are drawn into the cylinders are mixed by a carburetor or an electronic injection system (a modern version of the carburetor). While this is happening, the ignition system ignites the mixture with a spark from the spark plugs. The resulting explosion drives the piston downward. In each cylinder in the engine explosions occur milliseconds apart, which keeps the car running.

## The Fuel System

A fuel pump brings gasoline from the gas tank through the fuel line to the carburetor. The fuel goes through a filter to remove any dirt or rust before it goes to the carburetor (or fuel injectors).

The carburetor mixes the correct amount of gasoline with the air being drawn into the cylinders. Stepping on the gas pedal causes the carburetor to open, allowing more of the air-fuel mixture to enter the pistons, which speeds up the engine.

If too much gasoline enters the cylinders during cranking (while you're trying to start the car), the spark cannot ignite the mixture. This is called flooding the engine.

## The Pistons

Foreign and American cars have either four-, six-, or eight-cylinder engines. Each cylinder contains a piston. The pistons in the engine generate the power that drives the car. The combustion process takes place in four steps:

1. *Intake.* As the piston moves down, the fuel-air mixture is drawn into the cylinder through a special valve.
2. *Compression.* As the piston moves back up, the fuel-air intake valve is closed and the mixture is compressed against the top of the cylinder.
3. *Power.* The instant the piston reaches the top of its stroke, a spark from the spark plug ignites the mixture, causing a mini-explosion, which drives the piston back down.
4. *Exhaust.* The piston then moves back up, forcing the residue from the mini-explosion out a release valve, and the process repeats itself. The burned gases exit the car via the exhaust pipe and muffler.

Intake

Compression

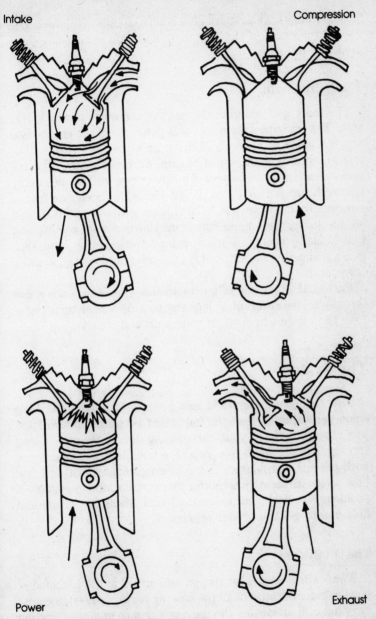

Power

Exhaust

**Pistons—the Four-Stroke Cycle**

Sometimes a weak spark plug will fail to ignite the fuel. This can be the cause of the popping noises you occasionally hear from the tail pipe.

### The Drive Chain

The more gas you give the engine, the more power it creates. The transmission moves this power from the engine (via a drive shaft in rear-wheel-drive cars) to the wheels. The transmission is made up of several different gears, like the gears on a ten-speed bicycle. The lower gears allow the engine to turn faster for the extra power needed to accelerate from a stop or to climb a steep hill. The higher gears are used at high speeds to let the engine run more slowly for longer life and better fuel economy. With a manual transmission, you shift gears manually. An automatic transmission does the shifting for you.

Part of the transfer of power to the wheels includes a differential. The differential lets the outside wheel turn faster than the inside wheel when you go around a curve.

# The Systems

Now that you understand how your car operates, here are some details on each of the important systems—information you can use to keep your car running almost forever. Going through this section *before* you have trouble will acquaint you with potential problems. The following chapter will tell you how to avoid them. Rereading this section after you have a problem will help you understand what could be wrong and help you to get the proper repairs.

### The Oil System

*What it does and what can go wrong:* Oil is the lifeblood of your engine. Because of all the moving parts, your engine gets very hot. Oil lubricates the moving parts to minimize friction and wear, and helps keep the engine cool. As it circulates through the engine block it picks up dirt and small bits of metal that collect inside the engine. With each pass, the oil goes through a filter that cleans out this debris.

Modern motor oils contain detergent and dispersant additives. The detergents, as you would expect, clean out dirt and grime from the engine, while the dispersants hold them in suspension where they can do little harm. This is what causes the golden-brown color of oil to turn dark. Dark oil means the oil is doing its job, not that it's ready to be changed.

Your owner's manual will tell you what kind of oil to use in your car. It will be described in terms of a viscosity index, a measure of how thick or thin the oil will get at different temperatures. Higher-viscosity (higher-number) oils are best for warm weather driving because they are thicker and offer better protection against high temperatures. In the winter, lower-viscosity (lower-number) oils are best because they are thinner and flow more easily, lubricating the engine faster in cold weather

The most common type of oil is 10W40. The "10W" means "10 winter." This oil will be thin enough for your engine to turn over easily in cold weather. The "40" is a warm-weather measure. The number 40 means that it will be four times as thick in the summer.

The American Petroleum Institute (API) grading system will help you judge the quality of the oil. The grades range from SA (the lowest) to SF (the highest) and include SB, SC, SD, and SE. These grades are stamped on each can of oil. Buying top-graded oil is one way to pamper your engine because SF oils have better antiwear properties than other grades.

Synthetic oils are a relatively new addition to the marketplace. In many respects they are superior to traditional mineral-based oils. For example, they are better at reducing friction, one of the most important functions of motor oil. In fact, they reduce friction so much that the manufacturers of these new oils claim that they will even improve your fuel economy. They are advertised as being good for thousands of miles (one manufacturer claims 25,000). Such claims may be valid, but they ignore an important role of oil—its cleaning properties. To keep the inner workings of your engine clean, you should change your oil every 3,500 miles. Because these synthetic oils cost two to three times as much as mineral oil, it doesn't make sense to buy them when high-quality mineral oils will do an excellent job of protecting your engine.

### The Cooling System

*What it does and what can go wrong:* Automobile engines generate enough heat to warm a six-room house in freezing temperatures. In cars with smaller radiators, air-conditioning, or crowded engine compartments, the temperature under the hood may rise to over 280 degrees.

In order to keep the engine cool, the engine block is surrounded by a blanket of flowing water that draws the heat away from the engine and into the radiator. Air blows across the radiator and cools the hot water before for it is returned to the engine. The diagram displays the various parts of this all-important system.

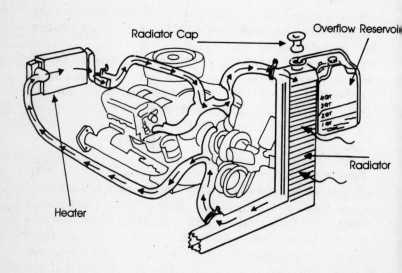

**Cooling System**

If the cooling system fails, the engine will become so hot that the parts expand to the point where they simply cease to move. Ironically, mechanics call this superheated condition "freezing up."

A properly operating cooling system is one of the most crucial elements in prolonging the life of the engine, yet it is one of the simplest systems in the car. It consists of a radiator, which spreads the water out so it can be cooled by the air; rubber hoses, which carry the water to and from the engine; the heater, which draws in the hot engine water to heat the inside of the car; the thermostat, which controls the flow of water through the engine in order to maintain the optimum operating temperature; and the water pump, which keeps the water moving through the system. (*Note:* Although I have used the term "water," in fact, the "water" is really a mixture of 50% antifreeze and 50% water).

When problems arise in the cooling system, they usually result from a leak. Cracked hoses, holes in the radiator, or a leaky gasket in the engine can cause a gradual loss of coolant until there is not enough to cool the engine effectively, which eventually overheats. A second typical problem involves a loose or broken water-pump belt, which stops the coolant from circulating through the engine.

When a water pump goes, you will sometimes hear the grinding of the bearings. This is often caused by a belt that's too tight or coolant water leaking into the pump's bearings.

## The Electrical System

*What it does and what can go wrong:* Your car has two main electrical systems. One starts your car and keeps it running; this is called the ignition system. The other provides electricity to run your lights, radio, and power accessories.

When you start the car, the battery provides power to run the starter motor, which moves the pistons so they can build up compression. At the same time, the battery supplies power for the spark plugs to ignite the mixture of air and gasoline that drives the car.

If everything is operating correctly, the engine, once

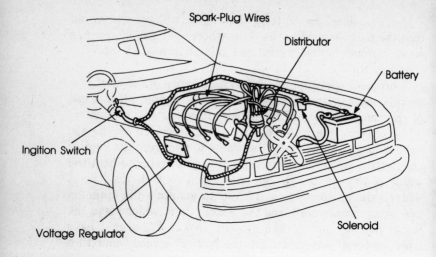

## Ignition System

started, will generate electricity for use by the spark plugs and other accessories.

Typical ignition-system problems include corroded electrical contacts in the distributor, which sends the electricity to the spark plugs; broken, cracked, or loose spark-plug wires; a faulty alternator that prevents the battery from recharging; and spark plugs that have outlived their usefulness and become clogged or fail to spark. Any one of these things can keep a car from starting or prevent the engine from running smoothly.

### The Battery

*What it does and what can go wrong:* Your car battery provides electricity for the starter motor and spark plugs. It also stores the electricity produced by the alternator or the generator. When you start up the car, the electricity passes through a coil, which increases the voltage, and then goes to the distributor, which sends bursts of electricity to the spark plugs at each cylinder at the exact moment of compression. Once the engine has started, the electrical system runs off of electricity provided by the generator (alternator) driven by a belt connected to the engine, and the battery is no longer needed. In fact, the battery is recharged by the alternator while the car is being driven. A voltage regulator insures that the battery isn't damaged by overcharging.

Battery failure is usually caused by problems with the alternator replenishing the electricity, low water level, corrosion around the cables, or age (although a well-cared-for battery can easily last five or six years).

Sometimes a car battery that is dead will start immediately if you jump it. If the battery is not that old, the problem could be dirty battery cables, so be sure to check them.

*Caution:* Don't smoke near the battery or expose it to flame or sparks. Battery acid gives off hydrogen, a flammable and explosive gas. Don't allow battery electrolyte (acid) to contact skin, eyes, clothing, or painted surfaces.

## The Brakes

*What they do and what can go wrong:* Your brake system uses hydraulic pressure to allow you to stop a 3,000-pound object easily. That is why a relatively light touch of the foot can stop your car, even when it is going 55 miles per hour. Stepping on the brakes forces brake fluid through a series of tubes that go to each wheel, pushing the brake pads against the brake drum or disks, slowing the car down. Drum brakes force the brake pads against the inside of a revolving drum, creating friction to slow the car down. Disk brakes work much like bicycle brakes, with the pads squeezing together around a spinning disk.

Brake systems can fail because the fluid in the brake lines has leaked out or because the pads are worn out.

## The Transmission

*What it does and what can go wrong:* The transmission is made up of a series of gears that control the power of the engine to your wheels. It allows the engine to function efficiently at high speeds and provides extra power for starting and quick pickup. Most cars sold in America have automatic transmissions, but manual transmissions are still very popular on economy and sports cars. With proper care, either type of transmission can last as long as you own your car, and at the very least you can keep expenses associated with this complicated device to a minimum. On front-wheel-drive cars, a single unit called a transaxle incorporates both the transmission and the differential.

As the name implies, an automatic transmission shifts the gears for you according to the speed of the engine and the power required. They are amazing devices and, as you can imagine, extremely complicated. Replacing an automatic transmission is one of the most expensive car-repair jobs, which is incentive enough to take good care of it.

Manual transmissions are much simpler because the unit does not have to figure out the right time to shift—you do. They are exceptionally durable and repairs are usually focused on the clutch. The clutch is operated by a foot pedal. It temporarily disengages the transmission from the engine while you change gears. Clutches go through a tremendous amount of stress, and they often need to be replaced during the life of the car. But they are not nearly as expensive to replace as an entire transmission. If a clutch pedal goes too long without adjustment, it will begin to slip, and the engine will race as if it were in neutral.

## The Steering and Suspension Systems

### STEERING

Many of today's cars come with some form of power-steering mechanism rather than a direct mechanical link to the front wheels. Power steering means that the steering wheel activates a motor to turn the wheels for you. Power steering enables you to turn the wheels easily in low-speed situations like parking.

The item in your steering system that is most likely to cause problems is the connection of the wheel itself to the steering mechanism of the car. Over time, and after hitting potholes and curbs, these connections will come loose. Your wheels may not be straight up and down, a condition called "toe-in", where each of the front tires points slightly inward.

SUSPENSION

The car's suspension system is what keeps you from feeling the thousands of little bumps in every mile of every road you drive on. The suspension system also keeps the car from swaying back and forth when turning, and from dipping up and down when starting and stopping. The front wheels of most cars are independently supported so that a bump on one side will not effect the other. Some high-performance cars also have independent rear suspension.

The suspension system is made up of springs and shocks. The springs cushion the ride by allowing the car to move up and down, and the shocks absorb the up-and-down motion to prevent too bouncy a ride. McPherson struts are combination shock absorber and suspension system. Replacing McPherson struts will be less frequent but more expensive.

## The Filters

*What they do and what can go wrong:* Clean air, oil, and fuel filters are vital to extending the life of your car. In addition to the grit, dirt, and other foreign matter that enters the engine and transmission from the outside, your car also creates its own contaminants through wear, condensation, and chemical reactions. Without filters, some components would not last more than a few miles.

The *air filter* is usually inside a large can or box on top of or next to the engine. It only takes a few minutes to inspect and replace the air filter. A clean filter protects the engine so that it can operate at maximum efficiency.

Here are some other filters you should know about: the *oil filter*, which traps dirt and metal filings, and protects finely machined parts; the *crankcase vent filter*, which prevents dirt from entering the crankcase; the *transmission filter*, which collects dirt and metal filings, and protects finely machined parts; and the *fuel filter*, which traps rust, sediment, dirt, and other particles that may enter the carburetor and clog tiny fuel jets. The *vapor canister*, which returns gasoline vapors from the fuel system to the carburetor, is also considered a filter. Changing and checking these filters should be done by a mechanic.

## The Belts

In a national survey of automobile mechanics, drive belts and hoses were classified among the most neglected parts of the car. Because these account for the majority of overheating problems, routinely replacing them after three to four years can add to the life of your car.

*What they do and what can go wrong:* The average engine has two or three belts. One belt drives the water pump; a second drives the alternator or generator, which charges the battery; and the third belt usually drives the air-conditioning. These belts, which are called V-belts because they are V-shaped rather than flat or round, may also power the air conditioner's compressor or, occasionally, an emission-control pump.

Drive-belt squeal and screech may be a cry for help. The belts may be telling you that they have grown loose and flabby. When belts slip, they cause overheating. That's because slippage causes friction, and heat from the friction may cause the belt to crack. The belt could snap—leaving you without a functioning water pump, power steering, or a battery charger (generator or alternator).

You can save yourself a lot of heartache and sometimes a lot of money by avoiding rip-offs on parts like voltage regulators, alternators, and batteries by simply checking the drive belts. Often there is nothing wrong with an automobile other than a loose drive belt, which in turn causes a starting problem, a weak battery charge, or another seemingly serious problem.

## The Windshield Wipers and Washers

*What they do and what can go wrong:* Your car has many important systems that depend on fluids. We have already described the fluids used in the oil, cooling, transmission, power-steering, and brake systems. The final fluid is one that your car doesn't really need in order to run, yet happens to be one of the most useful features of the modern automobile. All new cars now come with windshield-washing systems that spray your windshield with liquid at the touch of a button.

Not having enough fluid in the reservoir can be a safety hazard when you are on the highway and your car is covered with muddy spray, dried-on salt, or just as the rain is starting and your windshield wipers streak. Exposure to the extremes of the weather and normal use will age wiper blades, the rubber strips that actually wipe water from the windshield. "Chattering" noise and jerky motions usually result from deteriorated blades.

Depending on local conditions, wiper blades may need replacement in as few as six months; or they can last a year or more. Plan to replace your wiper blades annually if you regularly park outdoors.

## Fuel System

CHOOSING THE RIGHT GASOLINE

Is there any real difference in the various brands of gasoline? According to the gasoline companies, yes. However, many experts agree that most of the differences will not make a difference to you.

Premium gasolines do not burn cleaner or give your engine more power than regular gasoline. And higher octane doesn't give your car better mileage.

The one exception is gasoline with detergents that keep your fuel system clean. You've probably noticed that many of the oil companies are actively promoting detergent gasolines. The reason is that high repair bills associated with sophisticated fuel-injection systems have been attributed to clogged fuel injectors caused by gasoline. Adding detergent agents to

25

gasoline can reduce clogging and save consumers expensive repair bills.

Today most auto manufacturers strongly recommend the use of detergent gasolines with their fuel-injected cars. If you need a detergent gasoline, it pays to shop around. Some oil companies offer detergents only in their premium unleaded gasoline, which often costs fifteen cents a gallon more than regular. Other oil companies offer detergents in all grades of gasoline. By using a nonpremium grade of detergent gasoline, you can save over a hundred dollars per year. Remember: Detergent gasolines are *not* necessary for cars with standard carburetors.

What does a gasoline's octane rating mean? The octane rating of a gasoline is not a measure of power or quality. It is simply a measure of the gas's resistance to engine knock. Engine knock is the "pinging" sound you hear when the air-fuel mixture in your engine ignites prematurely during acceleration.

The gasoline octane rating appears on a yellow label on the fuel pump. Octane ratings vary with the different types of gas (premium or regular), in different parts of the country (higher altitudes require lower octane ratings), and even between brands (Texaco's gasolines may have a different rating than Exxon's).

Most new cars are designed to run on a posted octane rating of 87. This number is the average derived from testing each gasoline under two different conditions, low speed and high speed.

Use this simple procedure to determine the right octane rating for your car:

1. Have your engine tuned to exact factory specifications by a competent mechanic to make sure it is in good working condition.

2. When the gas in your tank is very low, fill up with the gasoline you usually use. After you have driven ten to fifteen miles, come to a complete stop and accelerate rapidly. If your engine knocks (makes that pinging sound) during acceleration, you should switch to a higher octane rating. If

there is no knocking sound, wait until your tank is very low and fill up with a lower-rated gasoline. Then repeat the test. When you reach the level of octane that causes your engine to knock during the test, go back to the next highest rating.

*Note:* Your engine may knock when you are accelerating a heavily loaded car up a hill or sometimes when the humidity is low. This is normal and generally goes not mean you need a higher-octane gas.

## METHANOL

Adding methanol to gasoline is one way to reduce the cost of fuel. This practice, however, is not without controversy. In fact, some car manufacturers specifically warn against using gasoline that contains methanol. They claim that adding it will cause poorer performance, deterioration of fuel-system parts, and poorer fuel economy. Other manufacturers indicate that a certain percentage of methanol will not affect your engine. Those companies that specifically warn against the use of methanol may not cover the cost of certain warranty repairs if methanol is used. Check the owner's manual for your car company's recommendation.

---

*Tip:* Since many states do not require gas pumps to display methanol content, ask the service-station manager if there is any (and at what percent) in the gasoline you use. Check your owner's manual and warranty before using gasoline with methanol additives.

---

## LEADED VS. UNLEADED

The Environmental Protection Agency estimates that 16 percent of gasoline users misfuel their vehicles with leaded gasoline, causing emissions of several pollutants: hydrocarbons, carbon monoxide, and nitrogen oxides. What many motorists don't realize, however, is that misfueling can cost them an additional 19 cents per gallon in maintenance costs and decreased performance.

Certainly all vehicles equipped with catalytic converters

should use *only* unleaded gasoline. Most engines manufac-
tured over the last decade have hardened valve seats and are
designed to run on unleaded gasoline only. They do not need
lead as a valve lubricant.

After an extensive study, the EPA recently said that "even
for those vehicles not specifically designed to operate without
lead or an alternative valve lubricant, the use of unleaded fuel
is unlikely to cause excessive wear under normal operating
conditions." Soon leaded gasoline will be virtually unavailable.


## The Tires

The tire is the single most complex item on a car. It has to
perform more functions simultaneously than any other part,
including bearing the load, steering, cushioning the ride, moving the car, and stopping.

Tire pressure is the most ignored item of auto maintenance
despite its effect on three different areas of auto operation:
tire wear, fuel consumption, and vehicle handling. Gasoline
mileage can drop as much as 0.5 percent for every one pound
per square inch (psi) of underinflation. Underinflation of the
tire by 4 psi can reduce the life of a tire by ten percent. Inade-
quate tire pressure can also make the vehicle unsafe to drive.

### TYPES OF TIRES

There are three types of tires on the market today: bias ply,
belted bias, and radial.

*Bias ply* tires are made with layers (or plies) of cords that
crisscross each other. These cords may be arranged in two or
more (even-numbered) layers. The more layers, the stronger
the tire.

*Belted bias* tires have cords arranged in a crisscross pattern
(like bias ply) as well as two or more layers of fabric or steel
"belts" over the cords. This increases the overall strength of
the tire. Belted tires tend to run cooler and last longer than
bias ply tires.

*Radial* tires are provided on all new cars sold in the U.S.
The cords in a radial tire run at right angles to the center line
and may be in one to three layers (plies). Over this radial

section lies a four-ply belt whose cords run at a slight angle to the center line of the tire. The result is a tire with a flexible sidewall (which is why radials often look like they need air), but with stiffness and strength in the tread. These characteristics add up to longer tread life and improved fuel efficiency.

*Warning: Never mix radials with other tire types.*

Snow and "all-season" are two subcategories of tires. Snow tires have an open tread pattern with deep grooves. Because snow tires wear out rapidly on dry roads and are inconvenient to change, the all-season tire has become one of the more popular tires on the market. The all-season tread pattern is effective in occasional snow, has good traction on wet roads, and will last longer than snow tires on dry roads.

Finally, there are retreads. In building a tire, adding the tread is the last step of the original manufacturing process. A retreader takes undamaged tires, strips off the remaining tread and repeats the last step of the original manufacturing process. Retreads can save thirty to fifty percent on the price of a similar new tire, and high-quality retreads will perform nearly as well. The National Tire Dealers and Retreaders Association (NTDRA) rates retread plants on a scale of A to F. A and B are passing, with A being the best. When buying a retread, be sure to ask for the manufacturer's NTDRA rating. Buying a retread from an A-rated retreader is an excellent way to save money.

BUYING TIRES

Most tires are sold at one of four outlets: independent dealers (large national chains and small stores that carry a number of brands), department stores (Sears, K-Mart, J. C. Penney), tire-company stores (Goodyear, Uniroyal), and service stations. Because the price of the same tire will vary from store to store, it pays to shop around. Check the sports section of your daily newspaper, where most tire ads are grouped together two or three times a week.

The most expensive place to buy tires is at a new-car dealership, with service stations a close second. You are most likely to find your best prices at independent tire dealers who carry a variety of tire brands.

As a way of helping consumers compare tires, the government now requires tires to have mileage and safety ratings. This little-known system grades tires according to treadwear, traction, and heat resistance. These grades are printed on the sidewall and attached to the tire on a paper label. In addition, every dealer can provide you with the grades of the tires he or she sells.

*The treadwear grade* gives you an idea of how much mileage to expect from a tire. It is shown in numbers—90, 100, 110, 120, and so forth. A tire graded 150 should give you 50 percent more mileage than one graded 100. In order to *estimate* the expected mileage, multiply the treadwear grade by 200. Under average conditions a tire graded 150 (times 200) should last 30,000 miles. Because individual driving habits vary considerably, it is best to use the treadwear as a *relative* basis of comparison rather than as an absolute predictor of mileage.

*Note:* For most of us high mileage is the most important aspect of a tire. However, few of us realize that where we live is a key factor in determining how long tires will last. In addition to construction and design, tire wear is affected by the level of abrasive material used in road surfaces. Generally, the West Coast, the Great Lakes region, and northern New England have road surfaces that are easiest on tires. The Appalachian and Rocky mountain areas are hardest on tires.

*Traction* is graded A, B, and C, and describes the ability of the tire to stop on wet surfaces. Tires graded A will stop on a wet road in a shorter distance than tires graded B or C. Tires rated C have poor traction. If you often drive on wet roads, buy a tire with a high traction grade.

*Heat resistance* is also graded A, B, and C. This grading is important because hot-running tires can result in blowouts or tread separation. An A rating means the tire will run cooler than one rated B or C and is less likely to fail if driven over long distances at highway speeds. In addition, tires that run cooler tend to be more fuel-efficient. If you drive a lot at high speed, a high heat-resistance grade is best.

*Tread design.* Look for a tread design that is made up of independent blocks arranged in a staggered fashion. These new designs have grooves that run from side to side in order to displace more water for better traction on wet roads. Most all-season tires have this tread pattern.

*Load range.* Check load range of the tire to insure that the tires are adequate for your driving needs. The maximum load is printed on each tire. The higher the load range the more weight you can carry. Add the weight of your car (in your owner's manual) and the weight of your average payload (passengers and baggage), and divide by four. This number should never exceed the maximum load printed on each tire.

# 2

# Preventative Maintenance: Extending the Life of Your Car

Preventative maintenance is the key to keeping your car healthy. While many automobile service problems are the result of faulty design and improper assembly, most mechanics agree that the single most important cause of today's astronomical repair bills and the premature death of automobiles is the failure of owners to conduct regular maintenance checks. Ignoring those squeaking brakes can mean the difference between a $79 set of replacement brake pads and a $475 brake job. A regular $14.95 oil change can prevent a major engine overhaul and add years to the life of your engine.

In the last chapter we discussed the various systems in your car and how they worked. In this chapter we will tell you how to check each of those systems and how to make them last. We have also included a summary of twenty key do-it-yourself maintenance checks to keep you on the road.

# The Systems

## The Oil System

*How to check it:* The phrase "fill it up and check the oil" has faded into gas station history. Today checking the oil is most often the responsibility of the driver. To check your oil, first turn off the engine. Find the dipstick. (Look for a loop made of flat wire located on the side of the engine.) If the engine has been running, the dipstick and surrounding engine parts will be hot. You may need a rag to protect your hands. Grab the loop, pull out the dipstick, clean it off, and reinsert it into the engine. Pull it out again and observe the oil level. You will note the words FULL and ADD marked at the end of the stick. If the level is between ADD and FULL you are okay. If it is below the ADD mark, you should add enough oil until it reaches the FULL line.

To add oil, remove the cap at the top of the engine and add whatever type of oil your owner's manual recommends. You may have to add more than one quart, but be careful not to put in too much. Overfilling can cause the oil to foam, depriving important parts of the engine of proper lubrication.

Many owner's manuals now contain instructions for changing the oil and filter. While you may be interested in changing your own oil, I don't necessarily recommend it. First, it can be a very messy job; second, you have to be prepared to dispose of the old oil properly (in a gas station receptacle); third, I recommend that you get the rest of your car lubricated *each time* you have your oil changed in order to prolong the life of the car's suspension system; and finally, the cost of an oil and filter change at specialty shops (which only do oil changes) and at gas stations can be remarkably inexpensive. You won't save much money by doing it yourself.

*How to make it last:* The most important thing an owner can do to prevent unnecessary engine wear after the initial break-in period with a new car is to ensure that the engine has a full supply of oil at all times.

Regular oil changes are the next most important thing you can do to keep your car running almost forever. Oil eventually "wears out" when its additives are depleted. When this happens, the various parts of the engine can be damaged. Sludge and deposits will build, and the oil can become too thick.

So, the two most important things you can do to make your engine run longer are:

1. Keep the oil reservoir filled.
2. Change your oil every 3,500 miles.

Because your oil filter plays such a key role in keeping your oil free of large particles, change the oil filter every time you have your oil changed. Buying top-graded (SF) oil is another way to pamper your engine. SF oils have the best antiwear properties.

---

*Tip:* When you get an oil change, have your car lubricated. Lubrication involves pumping grease into various joints and high-wear components of your car. This will help the suspension of your car last longer too.

---

**The Cooling System**

*How to check it:* Once a month or every 1,000 miles, whichever comes first, check the level of the coolant in the radiator. Whenever you tow a trailer or boat, check the level daily.

Coolant level should be checked on a cold engine. *Caution: Checking the coolant in a hot engine can be extremely dangerous.* Scalding hot water and steam can come out of the radiator.

If there is a chance the engine is hot, cover the radiator cap (see illustration, page 18) with a heavy cloth. Turn it counterclockwise to the first stop and let the pressure release. The pressure is gone when the hissing stops. Push down on the cap and turn it all the way around to remove it. (*Note:* When adding antifreeze/coolant, the proportions should be 50 to 70 percent antifreeze and 30 to 50 percent water. Do not use undiluted antifreeze as it comes from the container.)

Many late-model cars have a coolant recovery system. This plastic bottle attached to the radiator saves coolant that would normally overflow. It will automatically be drawn back into the radiator when the coolant cools down.

*Checking the hoses:* The top radiator hose (which generally needs more frequent replacement) is the easiest to check. It generally returns hot coolant from the engine, so it is subject to the highest temperatures. The radiator's bottom hose, which generally handles cooler water, is the supply hose. It supplies radiator-cooled coolant to the engine.

With the engine cold, physically check each one by squeezing it along its entire length. If a hose is soft and mushy or hard and brittle, then have it replaced.

Hoses should be pliable and free of cracks or swellings. You may need a flashlight to see some of the hard-to-get-at hoses. Look at the heater hoses, the smaller hoses that run back toward the fire wall (the wall at the rear separating the engine from the passenger compartment). Clamps holding the hoses should appear strong, secure, and free of corrosion.

---

*Tip:* Some mechanics recommend changing your radiator and heater hoses every two years. At the least, keep a spare on hand.

---

Four warning signs of cooling system trouble:

1. If you rev the engine and hear squealing, you probably have a loose belt.
2. The hose connections on the radiator look wet or you see greenish fluid under your car.
3.* The engine continues to run for a few seconds after the ignition has been turned off.
4.* The engine knocks or "pings" when accelerating.
  * (These symptoms also may signify an improper grade of fuel or need for an engine tune-up.)

*How to make it last:* Use a fifty-fifty mix of antifreeze and water in your coolant system. That mix is appropriate for most of the United States. It cools well in hot weater and protects well in winter. In certain frigid climates, you may need more antifreeze.

35

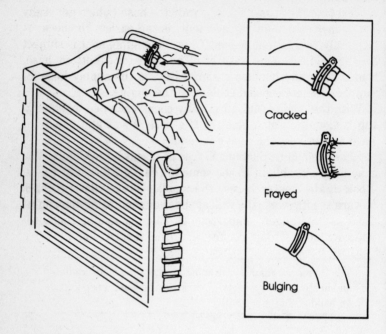

Cracked

Frayed

Bulging

## Hose Problems

Clean the radiator by spraying with a hose from the engine side. The bugs and so forth that get caught in it can reduce air flow and cooling efficiency. Look for fraying and cracks, too. Twist the water-pump belts arount to inspect them underneath.

An engine running above or below its normal operating temperature puts an added strain on the parts. If the temperature gauge on your dashboard registers above or below average, ask a mechanic to check the thermostat. Thermostat replacement is a quick and easy repair job, and an inexpensive item to replace.

Keep the proper tension on the water-pump belt to prevent it from failing. Press down on the middle of the belt. It shouldn't give more than about half an inch. Drain and flush the entire system as specified in your owner's manual to fight rust and corrosion. Most service stations have the equipment to give your cooling system a "reverse flush," the most effective way to clean out the system. Have the cooling system flushed and coolant changed at least once a year. If your car has been losing water or frequently overheating, you may have been topping off the fluid level with water. As a result the coolant/water ratio may no longer be fifty-fifty. Flushing and refilling the system will ensure that you have properly balanced coolant fluid.

## The Electrical System

Most of the components in your electrical system are too complicated to attempt do-it-yourself repair except, of course, the lights. A few years ago any car owner with a screwdriver could change any light on the car, including the headlights. That is still the case for taillights and overhead interior lights. But check your owner's manual or a local service station regarding your headlights. The new aerodynamic designs of today's cars are making headlight changes out of the reach of the average driver. *Note:* If the overhead light in your car goes out, first check the switch. It may be in the off position. The switch usually has three positions: completely off, permanently on, or a middle position that allows the light to go on whenever the car door is open. Look around the door frame near the hinges for a small button. This turns the light on and off. Push it a couple of times, as it may just be stuck.

*How to check it:* Check the fuse box whenever anything electrical in the car fails to operate. Like the fuses in your home, the fuses in the car protect the system from overloads and short circuits. The fuse box is usually located under or near the dash (check your owner's manual), and in newer cars each fuse is labeled. Know what type of fuses your car needs (check your owner's manual) and keep extras in your glove box—they could be a lifesaver.

## Spark Plugs

*How to check them:* Many mechanics use the spark plug as a simple diagnostic tool. The normal color for the spark end of the plug is light tan or gray. If you find the spark end is black, contains any goo, or appears to be damaged, it may indicate you need a complete tune-up or that you have a problem that includes more than just the spark plugs (though such plugs will have to be replaced too).

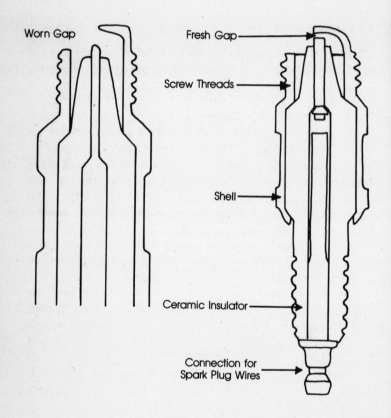

Worn Gap

Fresh Gap

Screw Threads

Shell

Ceramic Insulator

Connection for
Spark Plug Wires

**Spark Plugs**

*How to make them last:* A set of spark plugs can last as long as 10,000 to 12,000 miles on cars with conventional ignition systems and 15,000 to 30,000 miles on cars with electronic ignition. These figures are for optimum driving conditions. A new set of spark plugs once a year is a good investment to ensure fast winter starting. Changing spark plugs is easy, although it is not a complete tune-up. For less than ten dollars you can change the plugs in most cars. The owner's manual tells you exactly what type of plugs your car needs. All you need is a spark plug wrench, which is available at most department stores.

An important factor in the proper operation of your spark plugs is the distance between the two electrodes. This is called the "gap," and different engines require different distances. The proper gap distance can be found in your owner's manual, and it is measured by a special set of metal blades, each a different thickness.

The spark plug wires should be clean. Gently wipe them with a rag. Don't yank on them—you can crack the carbon core that carries the electrical current. Clean off corrosion around the terminals of other wires and tighten the connections.

## The Battery

*How to check it:* If you have a battery with caps on the top, lift off the caps and check to see if the fluid comes up to the bottom of the filler neck.

Check the battery cables. A common mistake is to buy a new battery when a new set of cables is all that is needed. Look for frayed or cracked cables and check for white, dusty corrosion around the connections. Finally, make sure the battery is clamped tightly in place.

*How to make it last:* Make sure that the battery has enough fluid in it and that there is no corrosion on the terminals or cables. Turn off the headlights and other power accessories when starting the car. Check the water level once a month. If it is low, add water (preferably distilled water). (*Note:* some of the newer batteries are permanently sealed and will not need water.) If the temperature is below freezing, add water only if you are planning to drive the car immediately. The newly added water can freeze and damage your battery.

Check the belt to the alternator for correct tension. If it is too loose, your battery will not get the recharging it needs to stay healthy. If it is too tight, you may damage the alternator.

Look for corrosion around the battery connections. Corrosion can prevent electrical circuits from being completed, leading you to assume your perfectly good battery is dead. Corrosion will also destroy the battery cables. To clean the battery terminals, first remove the battery cables. If the battery has top terminals, loosen the hex nut on the side of the clamps. If it has side terminals, loosen the bolt in the center of the terminal. Always disconnect and remove the negative connection of the battery before working on the positive connection. Do not allow the negative connection to touch metal while the positive cable is connected. Clean both the terminals and end of the cables with a stiff brush, steel wool, or sandpaper. You can use a solution of two tablespoons of baking soda dissolved in a cup of warm water. If the cables are corroded, clean them the same way. In addition to cleaning the terminals, cleaner will also neutralize any acid on the outside of the battery. Use the cleaner sparingly so that it does not get inside the battery or run down to the tray under the battery, where it can cause corrosion. Wipe off the cleaner with paper towels and immediately dispose of them safely so the acid deposits do not contaminate or damage anything else. When they are clean, tightly reconnect the terminals. Replace and tighten the connectors in the reverse order of their removal. Battery posts should be shiny when cables are reconnected.

Apply a light coating of grease, petroleum jelly, or protective spray designed to retard corrosion.


## The Brakes

*How to check them:* The most important safety item on the car is often the most ignored. A simple test will signal problems. (If you have power brakes, turn on the engine to do the test.) Push the brake pedal down and hold it down. The pedal should stop firmly about halfway to the floor and stay there. If the stop is mushy or the pedal keeps moving slowly to the floor, you should have your brakes checked.

Parking brakes let you know when they need adjustment. As linings wear, you must move the handle or foot pedal a greater distance before the brakes are fully engaged. Also, the cables and linkage should be lubricated when the parking brakes are adjusted.

*Checking your brake fluid:* The most important item in brake system maintenance is periodic checking of the brake-fluid level. Check the level monthly, or at least at every oil change. Many new cars have translucent brake fluid reservoirs in which the level can be checked without removing the cover. Check your owner's manual for its exact location.

On cars with opaque reservoirs, carefully wipe off the reservoir cover to remove any dirt before checking the level. Then pry the retaining clip aside and remove the cover. The fluid level should be kept about a half inch from the top on reservoirs that are not otherwise marked.

If you add your own brake fluid, buy it in small cans and store them tightly sealed in a cool, dry place. Discard open containers after one year. Brake fluid absorbs moisture, and excess moisture can damage your brake system.

Three different grades of automotive brake fluid are available. Using the correct grade is essential to maintaining proper brake operation in all driving conditions. Check your owner's manual for the right brake fluid for your car.

*Caution:* Be careful not to spill DOT 4 brake fluid on painted surfaces. It is a paint solvent, and it will quickly strip finished surfaces. DOT 5 fluid will not damage paint.

It is normal for the brake-fluid level to go down over a long period of time. However, if brake fluid must be frequently added, there may be a leak in the system. Have the brakes checked by a professional.

The color of brake fluid can indicate trouble. The fluid should not appear overly dark in color. If it does, it's probably old and overdue for replacement.

*How to make it last:* If you have built-in brake wear indicators, you'll hear a high-pitched squealing or cricketlike warning sound when it's time for new brake linings. The sound may come and go, or you may hear it whenever the wheels are rolling. It usually stops when the brake pedal is pushed down firmly.

As brake linings wear, you will have to push the pedal farther to put on the brakes. If you have automatic adjusters, they'll take up the slack and maintain proper pedal travel.

Brake linings will finally wear out from slowing and stopping thousands of times. When that happens, get a qualified service center to replace the necessary parts. Remember that the master cylinder, wheel cylinder, and all other components of the system should be checked at the same time. They may also be due for service when the linings are replaced.

Some car makers recommend changing the brake fluid every twenty-four months, regardless of mileage. This preventative maintenance can increase the life of any car's brake system. This service should be performed by a professional technician. In any case, check your brake fluid every month, or at least at every oil change.

Brake fluid deteriorates with age and will absorb water from the atmosphere. This could cause old fluid to boil in hard use, causing your brakes to fail. Old fluid can also cause the metal parts in your brake system to corrode and wear faster.

## The Transmission

*How to check your automatic transmission:* An automatic transmission is a very complicated item and expensive to replace. Checking your fluid level is easy and can prevent an expensive repair job. You will first have to find the transmission fluid dipstick. Usually it is at the rear of the engine and looks like a smaller version of the oil dipstick. To get an accurate reading, the engine should be warmed up and running. If the fluid is below the ADD line, pour in one pint at a time. Be sure not to overfill the reservoir. While checking the fluid, note its color. It should be a bright, cherry red. If it is a darker, reddish brown, the fluid needs changing. If it is very dark, nearly black, and has a burnt smell (like varnish), your transmission may be damaged. You should take it to a specialist. Automatic-transmission fluid is available at most department stores. Check the owner's manual or the transmission dipstick for the correct type for your car because the choice of transmission fluid affects the shifting characteristics of the transmission.

*How to check your manual transmission:* Always be sure the clutch pedal is loose enough to push down a half inch to an inch, depending on the car, before the clutch engages. It should require more pressure yet to push it to the floor. Have your clutch adjusted if the amount of play exceeds one inch.

Fluid levels in both the transmission and differential should be checked with each oil change, or when you notice erratic or rough gear shifting. Both are signs that the level is low. On most cars, the manual-transmission lubricant does not require changing but should be replenished if it gets low.

*How to make it last:* Automatic transmissions are more susceptible to damage than manual transmissions. One reason is that they are so automatic that we tend to neglect them. Another reason is that they are far more complex than manual transmissions. Here are some tips for making your transmission last.

### AUTOMATIC TRANSMISSIONS

Use the first gear (L1 or low) for hard pulling, snow, mud, or climbing steep grades.

Do not shift into neutral and coast. Driving in neutral gives no control over the car (it's illegal in many states) and is unsafe. If the engine should die while idling in neutral, the steering wheel could lock. Coasting could also increase the load on the brakes and damage the transmission.

### MANUAL TRANSMISSIONS

Do not rev the engine for more than ten seconds while the brakes are on.

Also, remember that low, or first, gear uses thirty percent more fuel than second gear. For minimum maintenance and maximum economy, shift from low to high as fast as you can and don't exceed the speed limit recommended for each gear in the owner's manual.

Chapter 4 contains more driving tips designed to extend the life of your transmission.

## The Steering and Suspension Systems

*How to check it:* Unless the power-steering system is leaking, fluid normally shouldn't have to be added. However, it's a good idea to check the fluid level every month.

Check the power-steering fluid with the engine at normal operating temperature, but not while it is running. The vehicle should be parked on a level surface with the front wheels pointed straight ahead. Locate the power-steering pump. Because it is difficult to find, many people forget about it. This pump, with its fluid reservoir, is usually on the driver's side and is connected by a drive belt to the engine. (*Note:* On some vehicles the power-steering reservoir is mounted away from the pump.) The fluid level in these reservoirs can usually be checked without removing a cap or cover. The fluid level should be maintained above the ADD mark on the reservoir.

Once you find it, wipe the dirt off the cap and remove it. Usually there is a little dipstick built right into the top of the reservoir cap. If not, you can tell where the fluid is by markings along the side of the reservoir neck. One way or the other, it's easy to check the fluid level, and if you need to add power-steering fluid, you'll usually need to add only a couple of ounces.

Check the hoses connected to the pump for leaks, wear, or chafing. If the hoses appear worn or cracked, have them replaced.

*Shocks* wear out gradually and almost unnoticeably. If the car sways on turns or tends to dip when you step on the brakes, the shocks have worn to the dangerous point and you should replace them. Worn shocks can also cause the tires to dance oddly on the road and to wear quickly and unevenly.

If your shocks are more than 15,000 miles old, do this check. Bounce the car up and down hard at each wheel. Once it's going good, let go and see how many times it bounces. Good healthy shocks will stop after one bounce. Weak shocks that bounce twice or more cause unnecessary tire wear and may also cause handling problems.

Your first tip-offs to misalignment are uneven tire wear and poor handling. An experienced mechanic can tell what types of alignment problem exist merely by looking at the tread wear pattern of the tires. He can also tell a lot by driving the car to see whether it pulls to one side or the other, fails to return to pointing straight ahead after a turn, or if it shakes or vibrates.

How long should wheels stay in alignment? Usually a year or more if the car has good suspension components and if it has not been subjected to heavy impacts or accident damage.

A wheel alignment will correct most steering and handling problems unless the parts are badly worn, the tires are out of balance, or the shock absorbers are weak.

One important do-it-yourself steering check involves standing outside of your car with your wheels straight ahead. Reach inside the car and turn the steering wheel while you watch the tires. The tires should begin to move at the same time you move the wheel. If you notice any delay, have your steering checked out—it probably needs alignment. Another check for misalignment is carefully to let go of the steering wheel when it is safe to do so and see if the car drifts to one side. If it does, you should have the alignment checked.

Proper alignment improves tire wear, steering, and fuel economy. A car with misaligned wheels has a higher rolling resistance and makes the engine work harder.

*How to make it last:* Shock absorbers will wear out gradually, and you can expect to replace them over the life of your car. To keep your car from becoming misaligned, try to avoid hitting potholes and curbs. You can prevent your power steering from prematurely failing by topping off the fluid (see above) and by not holding your steering wheel for long periods of time at its extreme limit during a turn when you hear squeaking.

## The Air Filter

*How to check it:* You can usually tell the filter needs changing simply by looking at it. If it appears dirty, change it. It is a simple task. If you are not sure how clean your filter is, try the following: When your engine has warmed up, put the car in park or neutral and, with the emergency brake on, let the car idle. Open the filter lid and remove the filter. If the engine begins to run faster, you need to change the filter.

*How to make it last:* Probably the easiest maintenance task concerning your car is changing your air filter.

This is how to do it:

1. Remove the air filter housing cover with a wrench or screwdriver, depending on fittings. Often the butterfly nut or clamps holding the housing cover can be removed by hand with no tools at all.
2. Remove the old air filter. If it's only slightly dirty, it can be gently tapped on a hard surface to dislodge dirt. If it is extremely dirty, discard it.
3. Check the small crankcase breather filter, if fitted. This small filter is generally fitted on the periphery of the housing. If it's dirty, replace it also. Unsnap the crankcase filter hose from its retaining clip on the filter neck.
4. Install a new crankcase filter. Snap the hose connector back on the filter neck.
5. Wipe the inside of the filter housing clean and install the new air filter. Replace the air filter cover.

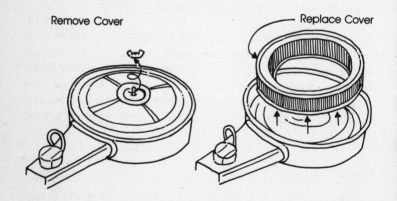

Remove Cover

Replace Cover

**Air Filter**

Be sure that the replacement air filter is the right one for your car. You need the make, model, engine size, and type of carburetor to buy the correct filter. An improper filter may fit the container but fail to protect the engine.

## The Belts

*How to check them:* Check belts by pressing down on the middle of each belt. A belt shouldn't give more than about half an inch. If it does, it needs to be tightened. Check for wear and cracks.

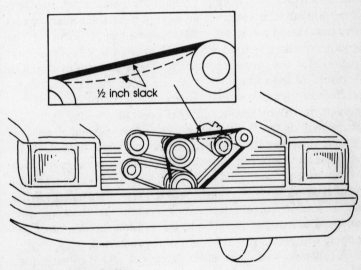

½ inch slack

**Checking the Belts**

To check the alternator-belt tension, grasp the vanes on the front of the alternator and try to turn them without using a lot of force. If they turn easily the belt is probably too loose.

*How to make them last:* Some studies have shown that belts more than four years old are likely to fail within the next twelve months. If one belt fails, it's best to replace the others at the same time or shortly thereafter.

When the mechanic either tightens a loose belt or replaces it, make sure that he or she uses a mechanical tension gauge to make sure he didn't tighten the belt too much or too little.

## The Windshield Wipers and Washers

*How to check them:* If fluid will not squirt from the washer nozzles, check for an inoperative pump, broken or kinked hoses, a clogged filter screen in the tank (usually located at the end of a hose attached to the cap or inside the tank), or clogged nozzles. Use a pin to unclog the nozzles that squirt onto the windshield.

The windshield-washer reservoir is a transparent plastic bottle located in the engine compartment. Sometimes it is very similar in appearance or located near the coolant recovery tank. Don't confuse it with the coolant tank. Some vehicles equipped with a rear-window washer use a separate reservoir mounted in the rear of the vehicle. These reservoirs should be serviced in the same manner as the front washer reservoir.

*How to make them last:* Keeping a mixture of windshield solvent in the reservoir will help prevent freezing, but plain water will do the trick of keeping your windshield clean. Buy fluid in the concentrated form rather than ready-mixed, as it is cheaper and more convenient than lugging around gallon jugs.

For winter use in cold climates, use windshield-washer solvent labeled for protection to –25 degrees Fahrenheit. Windshield-washer solvent loses its resistance to freezing when exposed to heat, so the solvent labeled for –25 degrees Fahrenheit will give a greater margin of protection.

A tablespoon of dishwasher detergent added to each quart of the solution will help if dirt is a problem.

Most wiper blades can be replaced in complete units of the rubber blade and its carrier. This method is the most convenient, but the most expensive. You can save money by buying just the rubber blade refill.

To purchase a replacement wiper blade, you will need the year and model of your car, the length of the blade and how the blade is attached. Installation instructions are usually packed with the parts.

*Tip:* Remove the old blade assembly from your car and bring it with you to the store to make sure you get the correct replacement.

## The Tires

*When to replace your tires:* When you insert the top of a penny into a tread grove, if all of Lincoln's head is visible it's time to replace the tire. While this old rule of thumb is still valid, today's tires have a *built-in* wear indicator. A series of smooth horizontal wear bars will appear across the surface of your tire when the tread depth reaches the danger zone.

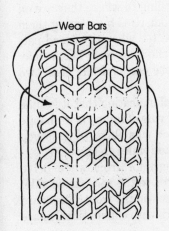

Wear Bars

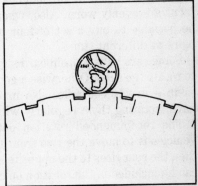

Insert a penny into the groove in the tire tread—the tread should cover all of Lincoln's head. If not, it's time to get new tires.

## Checking Your Tires

*How to read your tire tread:* Your tires can tell you a lot about how well you are taking care of them as well as providing important information about your suspension system. The following chart shows some typical signals your tire may be giving you and their probable cause.

| *If you see:* | *Probable cause:* |
|---|---|
| Wear on one side of the tread. | Tire is underinflated. |
| Wear in the middle of the tread. | Tire is overinflated. |
| Random patches of wear. | The tire is out of balance or wheel rim may be bent. |
| Wear on one shoulder. | Wheel alignment problem. |
| Circular wear spots. | You may have faulty shock absorbers. |
| Wear is in a random pattern. | The wheel camber needs adjusting or the wheel toe-in setting is incorrect. |

### TIRE ROTATION

Because tires wear differently according to where they are on the car, you can extend the life of your tires by rotating them on a regular basis. A car handles better when tire tread patterns are evenly worn. Also, when the tires wear out, it may be possible to buy a set of four more economically than two pairs at different times.

Some cars have a dashboard signal indicating that it is time to rotate the tires. Otherwise a good rule of thumb is to change them every 10,000 miles. No matter what kind of tires you have, rotating them regularly will add miles to their life.

The recommended rotation pattern for front-wheel-drive vehicles is to move the two front tires to the rear, same side, then the rear tires to the opposite sides on the front. The spare can be included in the rotation on cars with conventional spare tires.

If you have a rear- or four-wheel-drive car, move the rear tires to the front, same side, then the front tires to opposite sides in the rear.

# Twenty Key Do-It-Yourself Maintenance Checks for Avoiding Problems

A key ingredient in the recipe for keeping your car almost forever is your owner's manual. It provides you with directions to the many do-it-yourself checks necessary to keep your car going as well as your car's own schedule of periodic maintenance. The most important ingredient in making your car last is conducting regular preventative maintenance checks.

Here is a list of easy-to-do checks and tips that will help you keep your car in top shape. The first time you read it, you may want to have your owner's manual handy so you can find the exact location of the item mentioned. (*Warning:* Not following the recommendations in the owner's manual may void your warranty.) If you don't have a copy of the manual, try contacting the manufacturer at the appropriate address listed in the back of this book.

Remember that these are things everyone can do and they are very important for keeping your car in top shape.

1. Check the oil every 1,000 miles. Motor oil is your car's lifeblood. It is the single most important maintenance check you can make. To check the oil, find the dipstick, remove it, wipe it clean, insert it, and remove it again. The dipstick will show you how much oil you have. The oil line should be between the ADD and FULL marks. This check should be done when the engine is off, but warm.

2. Check the antifreeze/coolant level monthly. Most newer cars have plastic see-through tanks next to the radiator. Check the level markings. If low, fill it up with a fifty-fifty solution of permanent antifreeze and water. *Caution:* Do not remove the pressure cap when the engine is hot.

3. Inspect the radiator and heater hoses every two months. Check the clamps and look for leaks, cracks, and swelling.

4. Inspect belts monthly. Replace worn, cracked, or frayed belts. Push down on the belts and have them tightened if they have more than a half inch of slack.

5. Check the transmission fluid every 12,000 to 15,000 miles. With the engine warm and running, and the parking brake

on, shift to drive, then to park. Remove dipstick, wipe dry, insert and pull it out again. Add fluid if needed but be careful not to overfill.

6. Check brake fluid monthly, or at least at every oil change. First, use a rag to clean off the brake master cylinder reservoir lid. Pry off the retainer clip and remove the lid. If you need fluid, make sure you use the type recommended by the manufacturer. If you regularly add fluid, have a mechanic check for leaks.

7. Check the battery monthly. Make sure the cables are attached securely and free of corrosion. Open the caps (if your battery has them) and check the fluid level. Add water if needed. *Note:* Do not smoke or light a match near a battery.

8. Check the power-steering fluid once a month. Simply remove the reservoir dipstick. If the level is down, add power-steering fluid.

9. Check the air filter every two months. It's the easiest part to replace; it's right under the big metal "lid."

10. Check your brakes and parking brake monthly. First, push the brake pedal down. If it goes more than halfway to the floor without stopping, you have a problem. It should feel as though you are hitting something hard. If it feels mushy, have your brakes checked; there may be air in the brake lines.

11. Keep the windshield-washer reservoir full and replace your wiper blades when they streak. This check is more for safety than maintenance.

12. Check your lights monthly, including brake lights, turn signals, and emergency flashers. As you check them, wipe the headlights off with a wet rag. Also, take a moment to check your dashboard warning lights. When you turn the key one notch, do they all work? Your owner's manual will tell you which ones should light up.

13. Check your tire pressure monthly, keeping tires inflated to the maximum recommended pressure written on the side of tire. Give them the penny test and look for tread wear bars (see illustration, page 49). Check for cuts and bulges.

14. Test your shocks by bouncing the car up and down. If the car bounces two or more times after you let go, have your shocks replaced.

15. Keep a running tab on your fuel economy. A drop in your miles-per-gallon rate could signal engine problems or the need for a tune-up.

16. Periodically check under the car for leaking fluids and loose or broken exhaust clamps and supports. Look for holes in the muffler when the car is running. If you have a leakage problem, put three or four sheets of newspaper on a flat area and park your car over them. After leaving the car there a few hours, or overnight, back it off the newspapers and inspect them for leaking fluids. If the fluid is watery and greenish, it is probably from your radiator; if it is reddish and greasy, it is probably from your transmission or power-steering pump. Brake fluid would be light brown, and the darkest fluid is probably oil. Any of these leaks needs to be checked out. If you notice clear, clean water dripping from under your car, it is the normal condensation from your air conditioner.

17. Check for leaks after you wash the car (trunk, windows, sunroof, and floor carpeting).

18. Inspect your engine once a month for accumulated oil or grease. This could be evidence of a leaky gasket or oil filter.

19. Keep a log of all the maintenance work done on your car. This history can be a money-saving diagnostic tool. If a mechanic suggests that you need new brakes because they are squeaking, and your log tells you that they were recently replaced, you can intelligently suggest that you may need an adjustment rather than an expensive brake job. Most drug and department stores carry inexpensive car-cost logs.

20. Our final tip to avoid repair problems and to keep your car running is to resist installing major components after you buy the car. This includes air-conditioning, cruise control, power windows and locks, power antennas, and any so-called gas-saving devices. It does not include sound equipment.

# 3
# Trouble Shooting

To keep your car running almost forever, investigate any unusual noises, smells, or sounds immediately. A simple problem left unattended could become a major expense and hassle.

Here are some typical problems, what they could mean, and what you should do about them.

## What to Do When . . .

### You Feel Strange Vibrations

If you notice unusual vibrations when you drive, beware: There may be a wheel bearing letting loose, a drive shaft universal joint breaking, a transmission giving out, or a drive line part on the verge of failure. If the situation has developed suddenly, slow down, put on your flashers, and proceed with caution to a service station.

## You Smell Something Strange

If you smell a burning odor, it could be an electrical malfunction, an alternator problem, a loose hose, a belt trying to turn a jammed water pump, wiring trouble, a brake problem, or oil dripping on a hot exhaust pipe. A rotten-egg smell may be a sign of battery problems. *Warning:* The gas from batteries can be explosive, so be careful.

If you smell gasoline, stop the car and look for gas leaking around the engine, fuel pump, and fuel line. If you see any, don't continue. The hot engine could ignite the gasoline and cause an explosion.

The smell of burning oil could indicate that you're low on oil or transmission fluid. The smell of oil or exhaust in the passenger compartment might mean you have a faulty exhaust pipe.

A rotten-egg odor from the tail-pipe area while the engine is running means that too much fuel is reaching the catalytic converter because of ignition, carburetion, or mechanical problems.

## You Hear a Strange Sound

Most squeaks and rattles aren't serious. If you hear a new rattle, check the following possible sources before going to the service station:

1. Loose screws and bolts (both inside the car and under the hood).
2. Rearview and side mirrors
3. Dashboard knobs and trim
4. Radio speaker grills
5. Window and door cranks and locks
6. Ashtray (Is something inside? Has it been replaced tightly?)
7. Glove box (Is the door tight? Is anything in it rattling around?)
8. Hubcaps (Check inside for pebbles.)
9. Outside trim

Noises that are constant but slower than the engine speed, such as a tick-tick-tick, usually indicate a serious engine problem.

- A squealing sound can mean a loose drive belt. If the belt breaks, you'll hear a loud, rapid knocking sound lasting for only a few seconds.
- A loud roaring probably means a hole in the muffler. If the noise sounds as if it's coming from under the car, a mechanic can put it up on a lift and inspect the exhaust system for holes or loose fasteners.
- Whistling or hissing indicates an air (vacuum) hose leak.
- A wind squeal from windows that are closed may indicate that they are not closing fully and require adjustment by a mechanic to prevent leaks. You may need new weather stripping.
- Squealing brakes may mean the brakes need grease or new brake pads.
- Squealing tires probably indicate that you need an alignment.

**Your Temperature Light Goes On**

This is a sign that your engine is overheating. If you are stuck in traffic and can't pull over, turn off the air conditioner (if it's on), put the car in neutral, and step on the gas. Getting the engine to run faster will set the fan spinning faster. Finally, turn on your heater. Turning on the heat brings the heat from the engine into the car, which will dissipate it. If the red light goes out after you take these steps, you can probably go back to using your air conditioner when you start moving again.

If you are not stuck in traffic, pull off the road, turn on your flashers, turn off the key and check the following:

- You may have a leak in the radiator or one of the hoses. In either case, wait for the engine to cool. If the hose is leaking, tape it up. If the radiator is the problem, loosen the radiator cap one notch to relieve pressure, and drive slowly to the nearest service station.

- You may be low on coolant. When the radiator is cool enough to touch, check the level of coolant by carefully opening the cap. The liquid should come up to the base of the cap. If it's low, add water with the engine running.
- You may have a broken or loose fan belt. If the problem is the belt and the radiator is full, you can drive slowly until your warning light comes on again. Then stop and let the engine cool before starting up again.
- Check the fan. If the fan is not spinning properly, it can cause overheating. An easy way to check it is to grab one blade and spin it. If the fan spins more than four or five times without stopping, the clutches are gone and will need to be replaced.

## Your Engine Won't Start When It's Cold

The colder it is outside, the weaker your battery becomes, the thicker your oil, and the less volatile your gas. As a result, the starter turns the engine more slowly and the gas is harder to ignite, a combination that makes it difficult to start your engine. Consult the owner's manual to find out how many times the accelerator pedal should be depressed before turning on the ignition. It varies from car to car, but this strategy should solve the problem.

## Your Engine Won't Turn Over

If you turn the key, nothing happens, and all you hear is a click, the battery may be dead. First, however, check your headlights. If they go on and don't dim when you turn the key, the trouble may be with the neutral or park switch in your automatic transmission. Try jiggling the shifter in park or neutral while turning the key.

If the headlights don't work or if they dim when you try to start the engine, the problem is either a run-down battery or a poor battery connection. Use pliers to loosen the battery cable bolts (remove the terminal marked N first), pry clamps apart with an insulated screwdriver, and lift the cables off. Scrape the contact surfaces clean with a knife, nail file, or emery board. If you can reach it, also check the contact where the ground wire connects to the chassis or engine block. Now, securing the grounded side last, tightly reconnect everything. If your battery is not sealed, check the fluid level. (Don't smoke; explosive gases might ignite.) If the cells are low, refill them with water. If the car still won't start, you may need to get a jump start and have your battery recharged at a gas station.

Another suggestion is to remove your battery and bring it inside where it can warm up. Sometimes three to four hours in a warm spot can give the battery the strength it needs to turn your engine over.

### JUMP-STARTING A BATTERY

Most motorists have had to jump-start a car sometime during their driving career. Surprisingly, that innocent-looking battery can be the cause of serious injuries.

Batteries produce hydrogen gas when they discharge or undergo heavy use (such as cranking the engine for a long period of time). A lighted cigarette or a spark can cause this gas to explode. Whenever you work with the battery, always remove the negative (or ground) cable first; it usually is marked with a minus sign. When you are done, reconnect it last. This will greatly reduce the chance of causing a spark that could ignite any hydrogen gas.

For a safe "jump" start:

1. Connect each end of the red jump cable to the positive (+) terminal on each of the batteries.
2. Connect the end of the black jump cable to the negative (−) terminal of the good battery.
3. Connect the other end of the black cable to the engine block (or exposed metal away from the battery) of the car being started.
4. Now try starting the car with the dead battery. To avoid damage to the electrical parts of the car being started, make sure the engine is running at idle speed before disconnecting the cables. If the car won't start, the problem is probably not the battery.

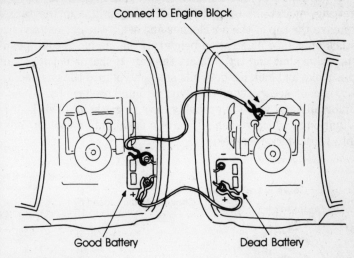

Connect to Engine Block

Good Battery          Dead Battery

## The Jump Start

If you can't get a jump start and your car has a manual transmission, try a roll start. Turn the key on, put the car in second gear and push in the clutch. Either push the car, or roll it downhill until you gather some speed (three to five miles per hour). Then quickly release the clutch and the engine may pop to life. If it does, push the clutch in and give it gas gently until the engine runs smoothly.

Still no luck? Call a tow truck.

### Your Engine Turns Over But Won't Start

If the engine does turn over but doesn't start and there's a strong gas smell, the engine is probably flooded. Check under the hood and make sure you don't see any gas. Wait a few minutes and then try cranking the engine for ten seconds with the gas pedal pushed all the way down to the floor. Don't pump it.

If that doesn't work, open the hood and make sure your spark plug wires are attached to the engine. Give each one a push to insure it is nested properly on the end of the plug.

If you haven't found the answer yet, your engine may not be getting enough air or gasoline. If there is gas in the tank, remove the top of the air cleaner and see if the choke valve is stuck open (see illustration below). If the engine is cold, push the valve shut and try to start the car. If that is not it, open the choke and look inside while someone pumps the gas pedal. If you can't see gas squirting, you've found the problem—and, unfortunately, you will probably have to get help. (This is one situation in which you should have a flashlight so you can look into those dark recesses.)

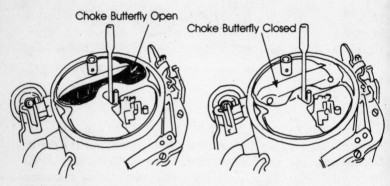

Choke Butterfly Open

Choke Butterfly Closed

**The Choke Valve (view with the air filter removed)**

### You Notice Liquid Leaking from Your Car

Clear water from the air conditioner is no problem and perfectly normal. Water that is brownish or green is probably from your cooling system and should be investigated. If anything else is dripping, however, it could mean something serious is wrong. For instance, red, pink, or light brownish greasy fluid indicates a leaky transmission. Black, oily fluid indicates an oil leak. You might be able to locate its source yourself very simply by cleaning the engine with one of the new engine-cleaning sprays, driving the car for a few miles, and then seeing where you have streaks of oil.

## Your Oil Light Goes On

If the warning light is working right, you've lost oil pressure and maybe oil, too. Pull off the road *immediately*, stop your engine and check the oil dipstick first. If no level shows, don't drive until you've added some oil. I know of many instances where an ignored oil light led to thousands of dollars of engine work. Without oil, your engine parts get so hot that they expand and jam up. This can virtually destroy the parts.

If your oil level shows full but the light stays on when the engine is running, don't drive any further.

If the warning light just flickers when you're stopped in traffic, your engine may be idling too slowly. Or your oil could be getting thin or low. Motor oil is the lifeblood of your car. Check it often. And don't go anywhere when you know you don't have enough. (*Tip:* Keep a quart along with a puncture-type can opener in the trunk for emergencies.)

## Your Engine Sputters and Spurts When Idling

One of the most common causes of a rough idle is that one of the cylinders does not work properly. In fact, if you have a large V-8 engine, you may drive for miles with one cylinder not working at all. Smaller, four-cylinder engines will run very rough when one of the cylinders is not firing properly because there are fewer cylinders. In either case, you are wasting gas and could be damaging the cylinder. Rough idle usually requires an inexpensive repair, such as cleaning or adjusting the choke or carburetor, or replacing the plugs and points.

Before you have any repairs made, however, open the hood and make sure your spark plug wires are securely connected to the spark plugs.

## Your Engine Dies While Driving

If you're not out of gas, it's a hot day, and you've been driving in stop-and-go traffic, you may have something called "vapor lock." Vapor lock happens when the gas gets so hot it begins to boil in the fuel line. The bubbles prevent the fuel from flowing to the carburetor. If this occurs, just wait. You will be able to start the car again after the engine has cooled off.

If you just splashed through high water, your ignition wires may be wet. Use a rag or paper towel to dry off the ignition wiring. If the distributor cap is accessible in your car, dry it off, too (inside and out, if possible). Try to start the car again. If the engine still won't start, simply wait and try again after twenty to thirty minutes.

## One of Your Electrical Items Fails

If anything electrical fails—light, horn, radio—the first check should always be the fuse box. Fuses can blow very easily, and you can replace them just as easily as long as you remember to keep a selection of fuses on hand in the glove compartment. Your owner's manual tells you what each fuse controls, and most fuse boxes are also marked with the information.

## Your Brake Light Goes On

Since 1968, all cars sold in America have two separate hydraulic systems that control the front and rear brakes. If you have a brake light, and it goes on, it means that one of those systems has failed. You should have enough braking power in your second system to stop the car. Test your brakes. If they still work, head slowly for a mechanic, avoiding the need for sudden stops.

## Your Heater Won't Work

If the fan is not working, check the fuses. Perhaps there's a loose connection or a faulty switch. Usually fan motors give a warning before failing completely. Check your antifreeze/coolant level—you might not be getting any heat if it is too low. If you have a temperature gauge on the instrument panel and it reads cool after driving for a while, have a mechanic check the thermostat.

## Your Window Leaks When It Rains

Make sure the rubber around the top of the glass covers both sides of the glass when the window is closed. The rubber may simply be out of place.

If that doesn't work, try putting weather-stripping adhesive under the loose portions or use a clear silicone sealer (it comes in a tube) to seal around the areas that are leaking.

Another alternative is to stick pieces of half-inch-wide black household weather stripping with an adhesive back into the trouble spots.

## Your Headlights Don't Seem Bright Enough

They may simply be dirty. A regular wipe with a damp cloth may clear up the problem. If oncoming cars flash their lights when you have your low beams on, then you need to adjust your headlights.

It is possible to adjust the headlights of some cars with a screwdriver and an owner's specification manual. However, a mechanic can do it in five minutes with a headlight aimer.

## Your Engine Knocks, Pings, and Sometimes Won't Shut Off

If your engine continues to run in a very jerky and unfamiliar way after you turn off the ignition, or has a strange knock when accelerating, maybe you are using gasoline with too low an octane rating. Experiment with higher-octane fuel before taking your car in for repairs.

## Your Alternator Light Goes On

If the alternator light goes on, *do not* turn your engine off. The light may be on because your battery is not charging properly. If so, you may not be able to get started again once the engine is turned off. Keep driving until you can pull into a garage or service station, or somewhere you can get a jump start. Keep your eye on the temperature and oil pressure gauges. The light might be on because of a loose drive belt.

## Your Seat Will Not Slide Forward or Back

First, look under the seat. A pencil or pen may be jamming the track. If your car is older, you may need to clean the tracks with a solvent. Then spray them with a lubricant like WD-40 (available in most department or hardware stores).

## You've Accidentally Locked Yourself Out of the Car

If you have conventional door locks on the car, straighten out a wire coat hanger and bend the end into the shape of a hook. Insert it between the rubber molding and the window or vent window. Hook it carefully around the door button and pull it up.

If your car has the new, smooth, cylindrical buttons, you'll have a harder job getting into it without a key. The hanger strategy probably won't work.

Calling a locksmith to make a "carcall" is expensive. Find out your car key code. The code may be on a small piece of metal in the center of your new car key (called a "punch-out") or on your new car invoice. If you no longer have the code, you might be able to get it from the dealer where you bought the car. Every car key is coded by the manufacturer, and having a new key made is less expensive and aggravating than breaking a window or having to pay the locksmith to come to your car. Keep your proof of ownership and the punch-out or invoice with the code number in a safe place. A locksmith or car dealer can make a key easily with your code, but only if you have proof that the car belongs to you.

If the car is locked but the trunk is open, you may be able to move the rear seat and gain access to the passenger compartment.

# 4
## Driving Tips to Prolong the Life of Your Car

## Tips for Breaking In Your New Car

Whether you have a new car or a car with a reconditioned engine, the initial break-in is a key factor in ensuring a long and efficient life for your car. In fact, a number of expensive repairs can be attributed to improper break-in. Even though your warranty may cover some of these expenses, problems resulting from improper break-in will often surface after the warranty has expired.

Here are some tips to keep in mind when you break-in your car. Following them for at least the first 500 miles, and preferably the first 2,000 miles, will substantially extend your car's life.

1. During the first 500 miles long trips are far better than numerous short ones. Vary the speed every few miles so the engine can break in at different speeds.
2. Do not accelerate rapidly during the break-in period. Also, do not decelerate rapidly from high speeds. For ex-

ample, suddenly letting up on the gas completely at high-way speeds can put an extra strain on your transmission.

3. Check your owner's manual for maximum break-in speeds. If your car has a manual transmission, the break-in speeds will be listed for each gear and are generally lower than the recommended speeds after break-in.

4. Do not warm up the engine. Keep your idle time to the absolute minimum. More oil circulates at running speeds than at idle, and you want maximum lubrication during break-in. (*Note:* In severely cold weather, it *is* advisable to warm up the engine, but only for a minute.)

5. Check your owner's manual for the number of times to depress the accelerator pedal prior to starting. The number may be different from the car you are used to, and you may flood the engine or cause the starter to work unnecessarily if you don't follow instructions.

6. Check your coolant level before you leave the showroom and after the first twenty-five miles or so of driving. Often the coolant has not been topped off, and overheating is one of the worst things you can do to a new engine.

7. If you have power steering, avoid holding the wheel at its extreme left or right. This will strain the power-steering pump.

8. Avoid using the air conditioner during the 500-mile break-in period. After break-in, try to turn off the air conditioner a few minutes before you stop the car in order to allow the engine to run at a cooler temperature.

9. Avoid trailer towing during the break-in period.

10. Remember that your brakes and tires are not as efficient during the first few hundred miles, so allow extra room for stopping.

## Driving Tips for Adding Years to the Life of Your Car

In addition to regular and preventative maintenance items, the way you drive can affect the life of your car. If you practice the following tips in your everyday driving, you will be making a substantial contribution to the long life of your car.

1. Never ride with your foot on the brake and always re-member to release your parking brake. Avoid the ten-dency to be a "two-footed" driver. Always use the same foot on the accelerator as on the brake. Avoid sudden stops, as heavy-duty use of the brakes will dramatically shorten their life.

2. Do not crank your starter motor for more than fifteen seconds at a time. Continual cranking will cause the starter motor to overheat, which will shorten its life.

3. Check your owner's manual for any special recommenda-tions for severe driving conditions. You may be surprised that "severe" driving is not long-distance driving at high-way speeds, but stop-and-go, around-town driving. Short trips combined with rapid acceleration are hard work for your car and its systems.

4. If you regularly carry heavy loads (in your trunk or trailer) and you notice people signaling that your high beams are on, you may need heavy-duty shock absorbers to keep your car at the proper level.

5. Start your engine before turning on your lights or other electrical items. This will direct all of your battery's start-ing power to the starter.

6. Do not use the temporary spare tire longer than is abso-lutely necessary. These smaller tires put an extra strain on your suspension system and can throw your car out of alignment.

7. Avoid letting the engine idle with the transmission in gear for long periods of time. Put the car in neutral and use the emergency brake, or shift into park.

8. Don't shift your automatic transmission into gear while the engine is running at high speed. If you feel a hard clunk when you shift, you're either giving too much gas or your engine is idling too high. A quick tap on the gas pedal can slow down your idle.

9. With a manual transmission, always push the clutch pedal fully to the floor when shifting. Also try to keep your hand off the shift lever while driving. If you stop at a light for more than thirty seconds, put the transmission in neutral, and take your foot off the clutch to avoid overheating.

Avoid "riding the clutch." Using the clutch to hold you on a hill or keeping the pedal slightly depressed will dramatically increase the wear on your clutch and shorten its life. Even if you have an automatic transmission, you shouldn't hold the car on a hill by slightly accelerating. Check your owner's manual for the proper speed for shifting manual transmissions. Using the wrong gear will increase fuel consumption and strain the engine.

10. Don't adjust your driving habits to compensate for changes in the way your car handles. For example, don't start pumping the brakes harder because they are getting softer or overcorrect steering because the car pulls in one direction. Have the problem checked out; your car is telling you something.

# Seasonal and Extreme-Weather Driving Tips

Extreme weather conditions can be the number-one enemy of your car. Here are some typical hazards and tips for keeping them from shortening the life of your car.

### Frozen Locks

If your car door lock is frozen, you can use a hair dryer to defrost it. Avoid open flames, such as matches and lighters, because they may damage the finish of the car, but heating your key this way may be helpful. Hot water, which works quickly, is only a temporary solution. Adding more water to the lock will only lead to refreezing. Periodically putting liquid graphite in the locks can help to avoid this problem.

### Snow on the Roof

If your car is covered with snow, be sure to clear off the entire car, including the headlights and roof, before driving. As the snow on the roof melts it can suddenly slip down on the windshield while you are driving. This presents not only a safety hazard, but if your wipers are on or you try to use them to clear the snow, they may break. (This happened to my associate on her way to work this past winter).

## Getting "Unstuck" in Snow

However careful you may be, you will probably get stuck in snow sometime. If you get stuck, try to avoid spinning the wheels. A single rotation of the wheels may be enough to get the car out of the snow under its own power. Put the car in gear and press the accelerator very gently. If that doesn't work, try to "rock" your car out by taking your foot on and off the gas (which is okay). But don't let the wheels spin for more than ten or fifteen seconds. When rocking, let your foot off the gas the instant the car stops its forward rock. Turn off all your accessories and roll down the windows so you can listen to the wheels.

If you have front-wheel drive, turning the wheels to one side or the other will often provide enough traction to get out.

## Supplies for Snow and Ice

In the fall, make sure you have the proper supplies in your car. Your equipment should include an inexpensive folding shovel, a snow brush, an ice scraper, and sand. (*Tip:* Carry the sand in plastic gallon milk bottles to keep it from spilling and make it easy to pour the sand right where you want. One bottle should be enough for most situations.)

Never carry salt in your trunk. Moisture causes salt to react with the metal or rug in your trunk. Sand is just as effective as salt and works much faster.

## Summer Heat

Keep tires cool in the summer by maintaining the recommended air pressure. Heat is the greatest enemy of a tire. Make sure to check tire pressure when the tires are cold because heat increases tire pressure readings.

## Rain

Slow down in the rain to help avoid hydroplaning—the condition that occurs when the tires lose contact with the road and ride on top of the water. Be particularly careful during the first rain after a dry spell. Oil and grease that has accumulated on the road will become quite slick after the first drizzle. This is a prime time for accidents.

## Saving Money at the Pump

Saving money at the gas pump doesn't necessarily require shopping around for the cheapest gas. Here are some ways to cut your operating costs that will also contribute to stretching the life of your car.

### Try to Avoid Short Trips

They are expensive because they usually involve a "cold" vehicle. For the first mile or two a cold vehicle gets just thirty to forty percent of the mileage it gets when fully warm. In addition to being inefficient, short trips *generate the most wear and tear on your engine*. A car driven primarily on the highway is far more likely to be in top operating condition than one with half the mileage that has been used for short hops around town.

### Tune Up Your Engine

If you notice a three-to-four miles per gallon drop over several tankfuls, change your driving patterns (see below) and make sure your tires are at maximum pressure. For maximum fuel efficiency, tires should be inflated to the top of the pressure range stamped on the sidewall. Check tire pressure when the tires are cold—before you've driven a long distance. If there's no improvement, consider a tune-up.

### Buy Radial Tires

If you need new tires, radials can improve your mileage from three to seven percent over conventional bias-ply tires. They also last longer and usually improve the way your car handles.

## Change Your Driving Habits

Adopting these habits will dramatically reduce wear and tear on your car (and save gas):

1. Accelerate slowly from a stop, as if you're trying to keep that morning cup of coffee from spilling off the dash.
2. Take your foot off the gas and coast (in gear) to a stop—it will reduce brake wear.
3. Use the cruise-control feature, if you have one, on the highway. It will keep your speed more constant and reduce gas consumption and engine strain.

## Check Your Thermostat

A cold-running engine will dramatically reduce fuel efficiency. Your engine temperature is controlled by a thermostat valve. Most engines are designed to operate efficiently at 180 degrees Fahrenheit. An engine running at 125 degrees can waste one out of every ten gallons of gas. If your temperature gauge runs cool or you feel your car should be getting better fuel economy, have your thermostat checked. Thermostats are inexpensive and relatively easy to replace. Running the engine at its proper temperature will lengthen its life.

## Avoid Gas-Saving Devices

So-called gas-saving devices should be avoided. There are literally hundreds of products on the market that claim to save you money at the gas pump. Not only do the majority of them fail to work, but some may even add to your repair costs. Keep in mind that no matter what the promotional material may say, to date no government agency endorses any of these products. In fact, the Environmental Protection Agency tests many of these products, and of the over one hundred products tested today, only six were shown actually to improve fuel efficiency. And these offered only limited savings because of their cost and relatively small improvement in fuel efficiency. None of the products are readily available, but the one that seems most common is a product that automatically turns off

71

your air conditioner during periods of rapid acceleration. This reduces engine drain and may increase fuel economy by 4 percent, but only when you are using your air conditioner. It is marketed under the names Passmaster Vehicle Air Conditioner Cutoff and P.A.S.S. Kit.

By the way, if your car has a catalytic converter, do not try to alter it or take it out. Not only is it against the law, but it may damage your engine or invalidate your warranty.

## Safety Belts and Safety Tips

There are two types of safety-belt mechanisms: vehicle-sensitive, which catch when the car slows down quickly; and belt-sensitive, which catch when the belt starts to pull out quickly. Test belt-sensitive systems by quickly pulling on the belt. If it doesn't catch, you may have vehicle-sensitive belts. To check these, put on your brakes while moving and pull on the belt. If neither results in the belt catching, bring your car to the dealer and have the belts checked. You should also have your belts checked and possibly replaced if they have ever restrained you in a serious accident.

The majority of people killed or injured in car crashes would have been saved from serious harm had they been wearing safety belts. Yet only three out of every ten Americans currently use these lifesaving devices.

Often people don't wear their belts because they don't know how safety belts work or simply don't know the facts about them. Here are some arguments that should help convince you to buckle up:

People mistakenly believe that they don't need a safety belt when they're traveling at low speeds or going on short trips. In fact, three out of four accidents happen within twenty-five miles of home. Accident rates are much higher on city streets than on highways. Eighty percent of deaths and serious injuries occur at speeds under forty miles per hour.

People fear being trapped by a seat belt and believe it's better to be thrown free in an accident. However, the chance of being killed is twenty-five times greater if you're ejected. A safety belt will keep you from plunging through the windshield; smashing into trees, rocks, or other cars; scraping along the ground; or getting run over by your own or another car. If you are wearing your belt, you're far more likely to be conscious after an accident to free yourself and other passengers.

It's not true that pregnant women should avoid wearing safety belts. According to the American Medical Association, "Both the pregnant mother and the fetus are safer, provided the lap belt is worn as low on the pelvis as possible."

Remember that no matter how good a driver you are, you can't control the other car. When another car comes at you, it may be the result of mechanical failure. There's no way to protect yourself against someone else's poor judgment and bad driving. Every one of us can expect to be in a crash once every ten years. For one out of twenty of us, it will be a serious crash. For one out of every sixty born today, it will be fatal.

At thirty-five miles per hour, the impact on you or your passengers is brutal. There's no way your arms and legs can brace you against that kind of collision. The speed and force are just too great. The force of impact at just ten miles per hour is equivalent to the force of a two-hundred-pound bag of cement dripped on you from a height of twelve feet.

*Tip:* Avoid cleaning seat belts with bleach. This could weaken them. Regular soap and water is best. After washing, keep the belts pulled out so they can dry. If your belts won't automatically retract, take a few minutes to see if you can correct the problem; if you can't, get them repaired.

## Avoiding Rear-Enders

If you are driving an older car that does not have a third brake light mounted on the back, consider having one installed. Inexpensive models are available in automotive-parts stores and, in most cases, installation is fairly easy. Most repair shops install the lights relatively inexpensively. Installing a third brake light will decrease your chances of being hit in the rear by fifty percent.

**Three-Point Safety Belts**

All cars currently sold in the U.S. are equipped to install lap and shoulder belts in the rear seats. If your car does not come with lap and shoulder belts, having them installed at the dealer will greatly increase the safety of your rear-seat occupants.

# Trip Checklist

If you routinely maintain your car, it should take you where you want to go without suffering breakdown. Here is a pretrip checklist.

1. Under the Hood
   Check all the fluids, including:
   [] battery water level
   [] radiator coolant
   [] brake fluid
   [] windshield washer
   [] oil
   [] transmission/clutch oil
   [] power-steering fluid
   Check:
   [] hoses
   [] belts
   Check and clean:
   [] battery terminals
   Check for:
   [] loose, broken, or frayed wiring
   [] loose screws, bolts, and other parts
2. Outside the Car
   Check:
   [] all lights
   [] loose trim
   [] wiper blades
   [] license plates
   [] tires for proper pressure, wear, and damage

*3.* Inside the Car
Check:
[] all the gauges
[] brake pedal for soft, mushy feeling
[] lights
[] horn
[] emergency flashers
[] turn signals
[] windshield wipers
[] spare tire
[] tool kit
[] for liquid leaks
[] loose parts

If your trip will take you to a different climate, remember to prepare accordingly. If you plan on doing a lot of high-altitude driving, stop off at a local gas station and have the idle and/or air-fuel mixture adjusted if the engine seems to be operating poorly. If you are going to colder climates, make sure your battery is in top shape.

# Your Toolbox

A small investment in some basic tools could mean the difference between waiting by a deserted road for assistance that may be hours in coming and a quick adjustment or repair that could get you back on the road. Even if you cannot make the repair yourself, a passenger or passerby may be able to assist you if you have these basic tools and spare parts:

| TOOLS | SPARE PARTS |
|---|---|
| *Screwdrivers:* | Fan or alternator belt(s) |
| Large flat head | Spark plugs |
| Small flat head | Cooling hoses |
| Medium Phillips head | Hose clamps |

TOOLS

*Pliers*

*Wrenches:*

    Medium adjustable

    Small crescent

    Large crescent

    Spark plug wrench

*Flashlight*

*Electrical Tape*

*Paper Towels or Rags*

SAFETY ITEMS

    Flares or reflectors

    Fire extinguisher

    Bandages

    Blanket

    Tire-pressure gauge

    Tire-changing equipment

# 5
## Looking Good

It's no fun to have a car that runs well but looks rusted and debilitated. Most car owners want their car to look good as well as run well. Not only will keeping the appearance of your car in top shape help maintain its value, but you'll feel better about your investment. It is amazing how well a car seems to run after a thorough cleaning, inside and out. In this section we will tell you everything you need to know to keep your car looking good.

## The Inside Job

First of all, there is nothing about cleaning the inside and outside of your car that requires special cleaning products (except the engine). What you use in your home will work just as well on the four inside car cleaning jobs: upholstery, dash and trim, carpet, and windows.

## Upholstery

A solution of one part household ammomnia and three parts water will clean most fabric upholstery. The key to success is not to get the upholstery too wet. Use cloth rags rather than sponges.

To remove stains from fabric upholstery, begin at the outside of the stain and work toward the center to help prevent a ring when you're finished. Keep changing your cloth as you work.

When the stain is clean, dry the area as quickly as possible. If a ring shows up, repeat the process. You can use a hair dryer to dry the fabric, but be careful not to burn it.

To clean vinyl car upholstery, all you need is soap (non-alkaline is best) and warm water. Vinly cleans easily. There are some special vinyl-cleaning products on the market, but soap and water works just as well. Be careful to rinse surfaces well and wipe dry, because soap can leave a film. If your vinyl is old and faded, consider using a vinyl reconditioner after cleaning it well.

The best way to clean leather upholstery is to wipe it with a damp cloth, followed by a thorough drying with a cloth. Use extreme care when cleaning perforated leather, because you don't want moisture to permeate the leather. For very difficult stains, use saddle soap and water. After cleaning with saddle soap, rub the leather with a leather preservative. Do not use fabric or vinyl cleaners on real leather.

## Dashboard and Trim

If you have a faded vinyl dash, revitalize it with a vinyl penetrant. A vinyl penetrant will restore the sheen to vinyl. You can find them in the automotive section of department stores or auto-parts stores.

Cleaning the crevice between the dash and the windshield can be nearly impossible. You can see the bugs and debris, but you just can't get to them. If a whisk broom or the crevice tool on your vacuum won't work by themselves, try them again while the defroster is on. If that doesn't work and those little critters are bugging you, consider buying a small aerosol can used to blow dust out of delicate equipment. Hardware and office-supply stores often carry these cans. These usually come with strawlike nozzles that will fit into almost every crevice in your car. Look out, bugs!

Door and window moldings need to be tended for reasons other than good looks. After a while, the rubberlike moldings around the doors and windows can grow hard and brittle. They are designed to seal out rain, snow, dust, cold, and road noise. Taking care of them keeps them flexible and functioning, as well as restoring their natural sheen. Spraying silicone lubricant on the weather stripping will prevent them from cracking and drying out and keep them looking new. You can get this lubricant at an automotive-repair shop.

If your seat or dash vinyl rips, you may want to try one of the vinyl mending kits, providing the rip is not on a high stress point. These products will not stand up to stress if the original vinyl failed. If the rip was caused by an accidental tear, they may work well. A temporary measure that is often good on older cars where color match isn't a major problem is colored vinyl or rubberized tape. There are so many colors on the market that you have a good chance of finding one that matches your seat. If the tear is very bad, consider buying a new seat rather than having the seat reupholstered. Look in the yellow pages under "Used Auto Parts" and call some of the junkyards near you. Who knows—they may have your exact seat in mint condition.

## Carpet

One way to make the carpeting in your car last is to buy floor mats. They are far easier to clean and much cheaper to replace. If your carpet does need cleaning, your favorite home carpet cleaner should do the job.

Before you attempt to clean stubborn stains, give the carpet a good vacuuming. Tank-type home vacuums with an upholstery brush and crevice tool are far superior to the little hand-held car vacuums that plug into the lighter.

To remove grease and tar, use a solvent-type cleaner. White

or gray stains on the carpet are most likely salt stains from the snow season. To remove them, you will have to scrub the area repeatedly with hot, sudsy water. A wet/dry vacuum cleaner will help to remove each load of water. If a cigarette burns your carpet or a small stain is impossible to remove, you can repair it with a piece of carpet from underneath the seat. Carefully cut around the bad spot and glue or sew the new piece in place.

To remove chewing gum, try hardening the gum with ice so it can be scraped away. Another strategy for nonfabric surfaces is to spread a teaspoonful of peanut butter on the gum. Leave it for fifteen minutes while the peanut oil helps loosen the gum. Then clean the oil residue with soap and water.

If someone gets sick in your car, first scrape and sponge the area with a cold-water cloth. Then wash with mild warm soapy water. Finally, wash the area with baking soda and water, (one teaspoon of baking soda to one cup of water) to deodorize the area.

For blood, use a rag soaked with cold water. Rinse and squeeze the rag frequently. Then use household ammonia cleaner to finish the job.

Chocolate should be cleaned with warm water and mild soapsuds followed by light rubbing with cleaning fluid. Nonchocolate candy needs very hot water, followed by a mild soap solution.

---

*Tip:* Before you try any new cleaning agents, test them on a part of the carpet or upholstery that is hidden from view. Do not use laundry soaps or bleaches.

---

## Windows

Any home window cleaner works on the windows and windshield, including a do-it-yourself mild ammonia or vinegar solution (four tablespoons of either to one quart of water). Use a clean, lint-free paper towel to get into the corners.

---

*Tip:* Don't wash windows in bright sunlight—it leaves streaks.

---

Don't forget to wipe off the windshield blades. If you have a convertible with a plastic rear window, it may become cloudy from oxidation. Check in the auto section of a department store for a conditioner that can remove some of the cloudiness. The sun oxidizes the window and makes it cloudy, so try not to park with the plastic window in direct sunlight for long periods of time.

# Keeping the Shine

While you can clean the inside of your car at irregular intervals, regular exterior cleaning is mandatory for making the exterior of your car last. Few factors affect the value and life of your car as much as the condition of its body. If your engine goes bad, it can usually be replaced more easily and less expensively than the major body parts ruined by rust and corrosion. Your best protection against the ravages of rust and corrosion is regular cleaning and periodic inspection.

### Preventing Rust

Not only is rust one of the most insidious hazards to your car, but a rust problem will depreciate the value of your car more than nearly any other automobile problem.

The key to preventing rust is to keep your car as clean and dry as possible.

Rust begins with a light brown stain. Don't ignore it. Have it inspected by a professional body shop. Heading off trouble early will save money in the long run, but if you miss the early rust signs and the problem continues, it does not mean that buying a new car is the solution. Major rust problems *can* be repaired. If you find rust on a chrome part, however, complete replacement with a recycled part is the most economical solution.

A major cause of car rust in the United States is the millions of tons of road salt used to treat winter roads. Acid rain is another factor—attacking paint and removing the protective barrier of the metal. Salt works its way upward, carried by moisture, into every nook and cranny of the car. In fact, salt causes car rust in *spring* more often than in winter because temperatures rise, inducing salt-caused oxidation. Likewise, leaving your car in a heated garage in winter can also speed up salt corrosion.

With all the fear associated with the potential rusting of your car, you might think you should get your car rust-proofed. Don't. Today's new cars come with good corrosion protection built in and good warranties against corrosion. In addition, the very act of rust-proofing a car after you have driven it for a while may do more to *cause* rust than prevent it—you may be sealing in the corrosive materials you are trying to protect against. Moreover, most rust-proofing programs involve drilling holes into various parts of the car to spray material inside those parts. Drilling these holes breaks the manufacturer's corrosive seal, and ironically it is in these holes that rust usually starts. In fact, some manufacturers, such as Toyota, specifically recommend against rust-proofing.

There are other problems with rust-proofing, as well: (1) you are probably paying for coverage overlapping your warranty; (2) rust-proofing often requires expensive inspections; and (3) some consumers have paid for rust-proofing only to find that nothing was ever sprayed inside. In short, rust-proofing is expensive and of negligible value. A better course of prevention is to keep the exterior and undercarriage of your car clean and have a good understanding of what's covered under your new-car corrosion warranty.

A word about undercoating: Undercoating is *not* rust-proofing. It is a sound deadener. If any moisture, salt, or other material is trapped beneath it, or if it later cracks, the undercoating can actually accelerate the rusting process.

To prevent rust, keep your car clean, wash it frequently, and wax it as often as you can. Hose down the underside every two months—more often if you live in an area where salt is used. Take care to rinse out the wheel wells and clean out leaves or other debris that retain moisture. Keep the drain holes in the frame, floors, and bottoms of the doors free.

Leave your doors open for a few minutes to let all the water drain out after you wash the car.

# Professional Waxing Instead of Repainting

If your car finish is dull, before you repaint consider a professional wax job. Repainting a car is very expensive, and unless it is done with a tremendous amount of precision and care, it won't be as good as the original job. Consider a paint job only if your car looks dull and lifeless and the streaks in the paint don't seem to come out even when you wax.

A professional polishing job involves rubbing away the top layer of paint using various rubbing compounds and cleaners. Once this is done, the nicks and pockmarks are touched up and the whole thing is covered with one or more coats of top-grade wax. A good "shine" pro's skill is not in the waxing but in peeling away just enough paint without destroying the color. You can often find one working out of car washes or gas stations. While the price may sound expensive, compare the cost of a paint job.

---

*Tip:* If your car absolutely needs a paint job, sticking to the original color will save you money and look better than a color change. Changing colors requires extra work on the fenders, trunk, and doors, which can be costly.

---

# Beware of Car Covers

If you park your car outside, you may have considered a car cover to protect it. But a car cover will not protect your car from moisture. In fact, vinyl, or waterproof, car covers actually trap moisture under the cover and prevent it from evaporating. A car with a waterproof cover will retain moisture all day, while one without a cover will dry in the sun after a rain.

Car covers are more trouble than they are worth. But if you decide you do want one, make sure it is 100 percent cotton so it dries out quickly and allows the moisture to evaporate easily. It should also be tightly woven in order to keep out the sunlight. Avoid car covers with metal grommets that can scratch your finish.

83

## Vinyl Tops and Trim

The best thing you can do to make your vinyl top last is to wash it regularly. Do not wax it. The abrasives in the wax can damage the thin coating of clear acrylic that protects the top and gives it its shine. To wash a vinyl top, use mild soapsuds, lukewarm water, and a soft-bristle brush. Regularly remove the residue so it won't be ground into the vinyl. After two or three years, you may notice dullness or fading in the top. If so, follow the regular cleaning with a vinyl top dressing available in most department stores.

If your vinyl top rips, cover the tear with tape until you can have it repaired. There are vinyl repair kits available to do the job. Choose a simple kit and be sure to follow the instructions that come with it.

---

*Tip:* Keep a sharp eye out for tiny bulges or bubbles in the top. They may indicate rust pockets forming under the vinyl. This is one of the hazards of a vinyl roof, and repair can be very expensive. If you find any bubbles, press on them gently. If they seem hard and crunchy, then rust may already have started. If they feel like air bubbles, carefully pierce them with a sharp object and try to squeeze the air out. If some adhesive comes out, wipe it off quickly and your problem should be solved. If nothing comes out or the bubble pops up again, use a glue injector and fill the bubble with glue. Then carefully squeeze out the excess until the vinyl lies flat.

---

## Washing and Waxing

Today's paint and finish jobs are better than ever before. With proper care, you can easily expect the paint job on your car to last for years. The key to long life is to treat the finish carefully. In general, I recommend washing your car monthly and waxing it twice a year. Because of the protective finish that comes on a new car, regular washing will be sufficient for the first two years of the life of the car. After the two-year mark, begin a regular waxing routing.

## Washing Tips

Hand-washing your car is preferable to automatic car washes. If you do use an automatic car wash, always use a brushless one. The big brushes on regular car washes can damage the finish, especially if it is very dirty and the brushes grind in the dirt. Also, avoid automatic car washes that recycle water. If you live in a high-salt area, then these facilities are spraying corrosive salt on your car. If you use an automatic car wash, don't waste your money on hot-wax sprays. They don't offer sufficient protection, and whether you use them or not, the car will need a coat of wax at least twice a year.

Always wash your car in the shade. Hose down the car first—this will rinse off the major dirt and cool down the surface if it is hot. High temperatures may cause the paint to stain. Wash with mild soap; household spray cleaners and laundry detergents may damage or discolor the paint or leave a film. Wash and rinse small areas of your vehicle at a time, especially on hot days. Start from the roof down and always spray the wheel wells and underside to loosen debris. Use clean, soft sponges or towels on the upper body. Loosen hard-to-remove dirt by placing a wet rag on it for a few minutes rather than trying to scratch it off. There are commercial products available to clean off dead bugs and other stubborn spots.

Use mild soap or dish detergent to clean the dirt and grease off tires. A scrub brush or scouring pad should remove stubborn stains, but be sure to wet the tires first. Never use gasoline or kerosene to clean tires. If your whitewalls are very dirty, you may want to clean them with special whitewall cleaner. Extremely scuffed tires can be painted with "tire black," which you can buy at auto-supply stores.

If you have a convertible top keep it clean by vacuuming or sweeping with a whisk broom. The metal mechanism should be clean and oiled so that it maneuvers smoothly. A coat of wax on the metal parts will help prevent rusting. Make sure that the well into which the top folds is also kept clean and free of debris.

## Waxing

Once your car is two years old, plan to wax it at least twice a year—even more if you can manage it. You can tell that your car is due for a waxing if water doesn't bead up on the surface.

The best way to protect the finish of your car is to use the two-step process—clean first, and then wax. After you have thoroughly washed your car, the first step is to deep-clean the old finish with a cleaner/polisher product. This contains a very mild abrasive that will clean off the oxidation and fill in the little scratches. After using a cleaner/polisher on the car, you must wax it. Because the cleaner/polisher leaves the surface exposed to the elements, the wax is necessary to seal in the beauty of the hard work you just finished.

While the two-step waxing process is the best way to protect the finish, there are also one-step car waxes on the market. These will not provide as deep a shine, but they are perfectly adequate.

Polysealant products, which contain polymer substances and can be found in the auto-supply store, are reputed to be more effective and longer-lasting than wax. These are the same substances that new-car dealers try to sell customers for several hundred dollars. Read the directions before you buy, as the application process is time-consuming. (You have to wash and polish your car before you apply the polymer.)

If you wax often, you really don't need a sealer. Although these products are reputed to retard the spread of rust, it's a good idea to inspect your car visually for signs of early rust.

# Body Work

If you need body work because of a major rust problem or accident, get it done as soon as possible. The practical reason for this is that you can stop the damage from getting any worse.

Minor scratches and dents require a different approach. To be constantly going back to the body shop with every little dent will add considerably to your operating expenses. You may consider waiting two or three years and have all the minor repairs done at the same time. The cost will be far less, and you will reduce the time your car is out of service. Between repair-shop visits, you will need to take care of any exposed metal. Regular waxing will help, and you should buy a small can of paint from your car dealer for minor touch-ups.

When shopping for body work, always get three estimates. This does not mean you should necessarily choose the cheapest.

Investigate shops recommended by friends or those listed in the yellow pages. Get a written estimate from each one.

While you are waiting for the estimate, look around at the cars being worked on. Looking at a body-work job before the final painting can tell you a lot about how well it was done.

Get close to the car and examine the area being worked on. Look for ripples, rough places, and bulges. When looking at finished work, resist the tendency to check the job by running your hand over the smooth paint. It may feel like silk but look horrible in the daylight. It's how it looks, not feels, that's important.

Make sure all the items on the estimate are written clearly and that you understand them. Will you be getting new or used parts? Used parts are fine, but make sure you're not paying new-part prices. When will the car be ready? What kind of guarantee is offered?

## Saving Money on Body Work

Used parts will be cheaper than new parts and may actually fit better. If many parts are involved and you have the time, consider finding the parts yourself at a local junkyard. Many body shops will be happy to let you supply the parts, as long as you can find the right ones.

Another way to save is to contact your local high schools, technical schools, or body-shop schools. The work, if the teacher is a professional, will often be first-rate.

If you need to replace some chrome trim and can't find an exact match, check with a body shop to see how much they would charge to remove the rest of it and fill the little holes used to attach it. If you have an older car, you may be surprised to find that this is a lot less expensive than paying for difficult-to-find replacement parts.

Finally, have the estimate divided into parts according to the type of work to be done: reassembly, body work, and painting. You may find that the painting at one shop is cheaper, so it might pay to have one shop do the body work and another paint it.

# 6
## Getting Repairs

Every car, regardless of the preventative maintenance you perform, will need repairs sooner or later. Not only is finding a good repair shop a difficult job, but trying to explain exactly what's wrong with your car can make getting good repairs seem like an impossible task. On top of that, you want to make sure that the repair was done correctly.

In this section, I will provide you with the tools you need to ensure that you get the best possible repairs. I'll also provide some money-saving repair tips, provide information on traditional repair rip-offs, and let you in on a little-known secret that will protect you against shoddy repair work.

Probably the first repairs you will make on your car will come during the warranty period, so we'll begin this section with a review of your rights while your car is under warranty.

## Warranty Repairs

Making your car last almost forever requires a good understanding of your warranty.

Every new car comes with two types of warranties: one provided by the manufacturer and one implied by law. Warranties provided by the manufacturer can be either "full" or "limited." The best warranty you can get is a full warranty. Full warranties must meet the standards set by federal law under the Magnuson-Moss Warranty Act and must cover all aspects of the product's performance.

Any guarantee that is not a full warranty is called a limited warranty. If the warranty is limited, it must be clearly marked as such, and you must be told exactly what the warranty covers. Most car manufacturers provide a limited warranty.

Any claims made by the salesperson are considered warranties. These claims are called express warranties, and you should have them put in writing if you consider them to be important. If the car does not live up to any of the promises made to you in the showroom, you may have a case against the seller.

The manufacturer can limit the amount of time the limited warranty is in effect. And, in most states, the manufacturer can also limit the amount of time that the warranty implied by law is in effect.

Most automobile warranties have a similar format. The differences are usually in the length of time or the amount of mileage covered, how the power train is warranted, and whether the car is warranted against rust.

Your car also comes with an emission-system warranty. The emission system is warranted by federal law. Any repairs required during the first five years or 50,000 miles will be paid for by the manufacturer if an original engine-part failure from a defect in materials or workmanship causes your car to exceed federal emissions standards.

Using leaded fuel in a car designed for unleaded fuel will void your emission-system warranty and may prevent the car from passing state inspection. Because an increasing number of states are requiring an emission test before a car can pass inspection, you may have to pay to fix the system if you used the wrong type of fuel. Repairs to emission systems are usually very expensive.

Finally, separate warranties are usually provided for tires and the battery. Options, such as a stereo system, should have their own warranties as well. The dealer should provide service.

Be careful not to confuse your warranty with a service contract. The service contract must be purchased separately; the warranty is yours at no extra cost when you buy the car.

If you have not already purchased a service contract, don't bother. Service contracts are bad investments. In most instances, defects in major components, such as the engine or transmission, should already be covered under a "warranty of merchantability." The companies who sell the contracts are very sure that on the average your repairs are going to cost less than the price you pay for the contract. Otherwise they wouldn't be in the business.

One alternative to buying a service contract is to deposit the $500 average contract cost into an interest-bearing savings account. If you have a major repair after your "free" warranty expires, chances are your reserve account will cover the cost. The greater likelihood, however, is that you will still have most of your nest egg, plus interest, for your next car purchase.

## Warranty Warning

If you have not already done so, make sure that any "dealer-added" options do not void your warranty. For example, some consumers who have purchased cruise control as an option to be installed by the dealer have found that their warranty is void when they take the car in for engine repairs. If you are in doubt, contact the manufacturer before you authorize the installation of dealer-supplied options. If the manufacturer says that adding the option will not void your warranty, get it in writing.

Most of us never read the warranty—until it is too late. In fact, because warranties often are difficult to read and understand, most of us don't really know what our warranties offer.

Taking the time to review your warranty before repairs are needed can pay off later by insuring that you get what's coming to you in free repairs. Warranties are difficult to compare because they contain lots of fine print and confusing language. You should review the actual warranty to make sure you understand the fine points. Remember, you have the right to inspect a warranty before you buy—it's the law.

The *basic warranty* covers most parts of the car against manufacturer's defects. The tires, batteries, and items you may add to the car are covered under separate warranties.

The *power train warranty* usually lasts longer than the basic warranty. Because each manufacturer's definition of the power train is different, it is important to find out exactly what your warranty covers. Power train coverage generally includes all engine parts, transmission, and drivetrain. On some luxury cars, additional items such as steering, suspension, and electrical components are also covered.

The *corrosion warranty* usually applies only to actual holes caused by rust. Read this section carefully because most corrosion warranties do not apply to what the manufacturer may describe as "cosmetic" rust or bad paint.

*Transferability* means the warranty will transfer to the new owner if you sell your car during the coverage period.

The *deductible* indicates how much you will have to pay when you take the car in for warranty work. Most deductibles apply onto to power train problems.

Finally, many warranties include your right to arbitration. If this information is specifically written in the warranty, you may have to use the program before filing a legal claim against the manufacturer. The law requires the program to be nonbinding on the consumer if it is written into the warranty. That means if you do not like the results you can seek other remedies. (See the section on Arbitration, page 115, for more help.)

# How to Choose a Garage and Deal with a Mechanic

Selecting a reliable repair shop involves two decisions. First, you have to decide what type of shop can best handle the work. You will not necessarily go to the same shop for all jobs; one shop may specialize in exhaust systems, for example, while another may be excellent at finding an obscure electrical problem. After selecting the type of shop that best suits your needs, you'll need to pick the individual shop and mechanic that offers the best quality service at a fair price. Be certain that the shop you choose for a specific job is familiar with your make and model of car.

Here are some tips to help you choose a garage and deal with your mechanic.

## Call Around

Don't choose a shop simply because it's nearby. Calling a few shops may save you up to fifty percent on the repair. But don't necessarily go for the lowest price. A good rule is to eliminate the highest and lowest estimates; the mechanic with the highest estimates is probably charging too much and the lowest may be cutting too many corners.

## Check the Reputation

Before you make a final decision, call your local consumer-affairs agency and the Better Business Bureau to find out the reputation of the shop. But remember, there are a lot of shops they've never heard of and others on which they don't have sufficient records. But if their reports on a shop aren't favorable, you can immediately disqualify it.

## Visit the Shop

When you go to see the shops, look at the mechanic's environment—the shop and the quality and condition of the equipment in it. This is a good measure of a mechanic's potential, although not proof of knowledge. A clean shop is wonderful. It means that the people there have clean habits, that when they work on your car they will probably be clean. But it's still not necessarily proof that your car will get fixed properly.

If your car is a '78 model or later, don't be afraid to ask outright if your shop has the right equipment to do the work you need. But beware—having fancy equipment doesn't mean the mechanic knows how to use it.

## Certified Mechanics

A "certified" mechanic is someone who has passed tests on car repair. Tests are prepared and given by auto manufacturers, oil companies, related industry organizations, or states.

The National Institute for Automotive Service Excellence (ASE) operates a voluntary mechanic certification program. Certification can be earned in engine repair, automatic transmission/transaxle, manual drivetrain axles; front end, brakes, electrical systems, heating and air-conditioning, engine performance, body repair, and painting and refinishing. A passing grade on the tests means that the mechanic is certified for five years. After that, he must renew his certification with a new test in each area. Beware: A shop can display the ASE sign even if they employ just one mechanic certified in only one tested specialty. In addition, the certified technician may not necessarily be the one who works on your car. There is a greater probability of encountering this situation in a large shop.

AAA-approved repair shops must offer engine tune-up, minor engine repair, brake and electrical services, and either suspension and steering or heating and air-conditioning services as a minimum.

To be approved, the shop must sign a contract specifying that, *when dealing with AAA members who properly identify themselves before repair work is begun,* the shop must:

- offer a written estimate that cannot be exceeded by more than 10 percent without additional member authorization;
- make available any replaced parts after repairs are completed, except those parts that must be returned to the manufacturer to satisfy warranty claims;
- guarantee its work for 90 days or 4,000 miles, whichever comes first;

• cooperate fully in any investigation of the complaint of an AAA member against the shop and abide by AAA's decision on the resolution of the complaint.

## Talking with a Mechanic

To get the best results from a mechanic, show interest in the problem. Don't hesitate to ask for an explanation of what's wrong with your car. You'll be surprised at how helpful a mechanic becomes just knowing that you're interested. Don't act like an expert. If you don't really understand what's wrong with your car, don't pretend that you do. It may only demonstrate your ignorance, setting you up to be taken by a dishonest mechanic. Express your satisfaction. If you're happy with the work, compliment the mechanic and ask for him or her the next time you come in. You'll get to know each other, and the mechanic will get to know your car. *Tip:* A good mechanic is a good diagnostician and should be able to tell you in plain English what is wrong with your car.

## Let the Mechanic Diagnose the Symptoms

Don't tell him what you think is wrong—you might be wrong yourself. Tell him the symptoms—what the car is (or isn't) doing that made you bring it in. Let him or her determine the cause. Tell what happens. Be specific. Does it happen all the time? Does it get worse or better under certain circumstances? Going fast or slow? While the engine was cold or hot? Did it start gradually or all at once? Any unusual noises? With this information, and possibly a test drive, a good mechanic will have a much better chance of pinpointing the ailment. On the other hand, trying to tell the mechanic what's wrong may send him off in the wrong direction.

Here is a list of questions from the AAA that will assist you in making helpful observations for the service technician.

1. How did you notice the problem?
   Smell    See    Hear    Feel
2. Can you make the problem occur whenever you want to demonstrate it to someone else?
3. Does the problem occur constantly or intermittently? Im-

mediately after starting the engine or after _____ miles or _____ minutes?

4. Do any of the instrument-panel gauges or warning lights react? Which instrument? Which light? What reaction?

5. What systems on the car are being operated when you notice the problem?

| | | |
|---|---|---|
| Starter | Turn Signals | Cruise Control |
| Gear Shift | Wiper/Washers | Air-Conditioning |
| Clutch | Radio | Rear-Window Defroster |
| Brakes | Heater | Other Accessory |

6. Does the problem occur when the engine is:

Cold     Warming up     Hot     Overheated

7. Does the problem change when engine speed changes and car speed remains same? Does the problem change when car speed changes and engine speed remains same?

8. What is the weather like when the problem occurs? All kinds of weather? Or only in certain weather (Clear, rainy/snowy, foggy, low humidity, high humidity, above a certain temperature, below a certain temperature, in a specific temperature range)?

9. Does the problem occur when the car is:

| | |
|---|---|
| Idling | Decelerating with brake |
| Accelerating | Maintaining constant speed |
| Between speeds of _____ and _____ | |
| At any speed In gear | |
| Being shifted from _____ to _____ gear | |
| On a rough road | Going uphill |
| On a smooth road | On a level road |
| Turning a sharp corner | Going downhill |
| Taking a gentle curve | Pulling a trailer |

10. Where do the symptoms seem to be coming from in the car?

Outside the passenger compartment

Right side     Left side     Front          Rear

Under the hood    In the trunk    Under the car
Inside the passenger compartment    Dashboard
Floor    Seat
Roof    Window

## Be Sensitive to Your Mechanic

Try to call for an appointment. It is much better if you have an appointment, and better yet if you can request work on Tuesday, Wednesday, or Thursday, that is, a day in the middle of the week. Most people decide to bring their car in on Monday or Friday. Monday because they had trouble on the weekend, and Friday because they would like it fixed in time for their days off. When a middle-of-the-week appointment can be scheduled, the mechanic may have more time to do the job, and chances are you'll get better results. Arrange ahead of time just how long the shop will need the car, and try to allow as much time as possible not only to repair the car, but also to road-test it to make sure the job was done properly. Do not stand over the mechanic's shoulder because you are in a hurry. Try to plan for some alternative means of transportation when the car is in the shop.

## Get Several Estimates

Auto repair is a competitive business, and prices can vary. Have each mechanic tell you what will be done for the price.

If you sign a service order, make sure it has relatively specific instructions. Be wary of blanket statements such as "Fix brakes" or "Repair engine." You could wind up with a complete brake job or new engine. Never sign a blank order, and never tell the shop personnel to "do what is necessary" unless the problem will clearly be covered by warranty. Instead, ask exactly what is being done and how much it will cost. Make sure the shop will call you if the work will exceed the estimate or if they are not sure how much work will be necessary. Put your telephone number on the repair order. Tell the service person you would like to have any replaced parts when you return to pick up the car; most good shops will comply with this unless the parts must be returned to the manufacturer for warranty or sent to a specialist for rebuilding. However, you still have a right to see them before they are sent away. Don't forget to have the person who writes the estimate sign it and get a copy for yourself.

A written estimate is very important. It's the best safeguard against the "five-o'clock surprise"—paying more than you expected. Check the estimate closely. Make sure each repair item is listed separately. If a tune-up is involved, be sure you know precisely what a tune-up includes.

## Repair Rip-Offs

Beware of mechanics who find problems with your car that are not obvious to you while you are driving. They will tell you about worn shocks, unsafe tires, leaky radiators, misaligned front ends, or other parts you ought to fix before they get worse. Take their advice—when you get home. Do not give a stranger a big job. Have someone you trust check it out.

The best protection against repair rip-off on the road is to have your car thoroughly checked before leaving on a trip and have on board the tools and parts necessary to fix disabling but not serious problems such as a broken fan belt, flat tires, or blown fuses.

Here are a few of the "dirty tricks" of the disreputable repair shops to watch out for:

- While checking under the hood, the attendant cuts the fan belt so that it hangs by a thread.
- A seltzer tablet is plunked into a battery cell, neutralizing some of the acid and causing it to boil over, making it look as if your battery needs work.
- The attendant doesn't push the dipstick all the way down when checking the oil and advises you that you need to add a quart.
- The attendant squirts oil on a shock absorber to make you think the seal is broken.
- While checking the air pressure, the attendant punctures your tire with a sharp tool.

- The attendant may tell you that the oil filter is terribly hot and it needs replacing. Don't believe it.

## Saving Money on Repairs

Saving money on car repairs is not easy, but certainly possible. Here are five strategies to minimize your repair bills:

1. Develop a "sider": If you get to know a mechanic employed by a repair shop, don't be afraid to ask if he is available for work on the side—evenings or weekends. The labor will be cheaper.
2. Independent diagnostic centers: One of the major problems in getting repairs done for the lowest price is that a repair shop has a built-in incentive to perform work that may not be necessary. If you suspect a major problem with your car, first take it to an independent diagnostic center. These facilities are not associated with repair shops, so they have no incentive to suggest repairs that are not really needed. The AAA runs many of these centers, and the charge is around $30 to $45. These diagnostic centers are also very useful for getting an unbiased opinion in settling a repair problem.
3. Double up for service and savings: A fact that most motorists overlook is that most car systems are interrelated, and servicing one is a good excuse for servicing another—and can save you money. The next time you take your car in for service on one of these items—consider the suggestion that follows.
   - Whenever the plugs are removed: Check compression.
   - Whenever the distributor is opened: Check cap and rotor. Clean and lubricate.
   - Whenever the intake manifold is removed: Replace lifters and change gasket.
   - Whenever the rocker cover is removed: Adjust lifters, if possible. Check the underside for varnish build-up (means too few oil changes).
   - Whenever the radiator is serviced: Replace all worn hoses and thermostat. Change fluid. Flush radiator. Check water pump. Perform a pressure test.

- Whenever the battery is serviced: Clean connections, add water, charge. Check hold-down bolt.
- Whenever the starter is serviced: Clean connections and check flywheel.
- Whenever the air-conditioning is serviced: Purge system and replenish refrigerant.
- Whenever the wheels are removed: Check (and service, if necessary) brakes, front bearings, front suspension, hand brake, shocks.
- Whenever the wheels are aligned: Check front suspension.
- Whenever the tires are changed: Have valve tested and wheel rims balanced.
- Whenever the exhaust is serviced: Check condition of hangers.
- Whenever the car is on a hoist: Check frame, floor pan, and fluid lines for rust.
- Whenever body work is done: Have replacement parts zinc-primed and painted.

4. Use rebuilt and used parts: Buying a rebuilt part (one that matches the original specifications and has been totally overhauled) can save as much as seventy-five percent of the cost of a brand-new part. When having repairs done, ask about rebuilt parts and the guarantee that comes with them. Used parts from a junkyard, too, may be perfectly good and cost one tenth what a new part would cost.

5. Use vocational school and high school facilities: Contact your local school system and see if they accept cars for repair. Many times your only cost will be parts, and the work is generally as good as you'll find anywhere.

## Tune-Ups

Few terms in the car-repair world are more misused than the term "tune-up." There are probably as many definitions for the word as there are mechanics who perform them. In addition, there are as many problems that a tune-up will supposedly correct as there are repair shops offering the service.

Because of extensive use of electronic controls, the old-fashioned engine tune-up that once entailed changing the breaker points, the plugs, and the distributor cap and setting the timing now consists mainly of changing the plugs, checking the timing, and replacing the air and gas filters.

Car companies generally recommend a tune-up every 30,000 miles, but hard driving may require one sooner. For example, many mechanics recommend a tune-up every 15,000 miles under normal driving conditions and every 10,000 miles under severe conditions.

A tune-up is a good investment in preventative maintenance that pays off—you'll have a reliable, smooth-running car. How do you know when you car needs a tune-up? One of the first things to do is to keep a running check on your gasoline mileage. If you know your average mileage per gallon (check over three tankfuls), when the miles-per-gallon average drops by over fifteen percent, chances are you need a tune-up and maybe some other work, too. Other symptoms of an out-of-tune engine are:

- idling too fast when the car is warm
- stalling
- low power
- rough idling
- knocking or pinging
- hard starting, misfiring, hesitation, or rough running
- the engine continuing to run with the key off
- black exhaust smoke

Remember, however, that experiencing these problems is no guarantee that you need an expensive tune-up. For example, a common problem is the idle speed: too low, the car can stall; too high, the engine continues to run even after the key is turned off. Often a mechanic can adjust the idle speed quickly with very simple tools and a couple of dollars' worth in parts. Ignition timing is another typical problem. This is often the culprit when you experience hard starting, pinging under acceleration, or loss of power. Like the idle speed, ignition timing can often be adjusted inexpensively.

Explain the symptoms and ask the mechanic to check the

engine before replacing anything. If a few minor adjustments can do the job, there is no reason for you to pay for a lot of unnecessary parts. If your engine is running well once those adjustments are made, forget replacing major parts. But keep a constant check, making sure the idle and ignition are okay. A bad case of pinging can literally cause your engine to disintegrate over a period of time.

A complete tune-up consists of at least four steps:

1. Checking cylinder compression to determine whether a mechanical problem exists that a simple tune-up would not help.
2. Checking the full ignition system and the carburetion and pollution systems against the specifications set down by the manufacturer.
3. Checking the engine-idle speed, ignition timing, vacuum, mechanical advance, points dwell, plugs, condenser, distributor cap, rotor, ignition coil, spark plug wires, and the PCV system with engine-testing equipment. The PCV, air filters, battery, automatic choke, and vacuum hoses can be checked visually.
4. All filters should be changed regularly, even between tune-ups. They get dirty and can harm the engine. Check them visually and change them regularly.

Finally, a good mechanic will clean the carburetor before beginning the adjustments. There is no point in adjusting a dirty carburetor.

## Using Your Credit Card to Resolve Repair Problems

If you are having problems with an auto mechanic, paying auto-repair bills by credit card can provide help in getting the problem resolved.

For example: Suppose you take your car to the mechanic because of a noise in the power steering. The shop does a rack-and-pinion overhaul. You pay $180 with your credit card and drive home. The next afternoon, the noise is back. Another mechanic looks at the car and finds that the real problem was fluid leaking from the power-steering pump. That will cost another $125 to repair.

What happens if the first mechanic refuses to make good on his mistake? If you had paid the bill with cash, you would be out $180 and might have to file suit to recover your money. If you paid by check, it would probably be too late to stop payment. Payment with a credit card not only gives you extra time, but is also an effective tool for negotiating with the mechanic.

According to federal law, you have the right to withhold payment for sloppy or incorrect repairs. Of course, you may withhold no more than the amount of the specific disputed repair.

In order to use this right, you must first try to work out the problem with the mechanic. Also, unless the credit-card company owns the repair shop (this might be the case with gasoline credit cards used at gas stations), two other conditions must be met: the repair shop must be in your home state (or within one hundred miles of your current address) and the cost of repairs must be over fifty dollars.

Until the problem is settled or resolved in court, the credit-card company cannot charge you interest or penalties on the amount in dispute.

If you decide to take such action, send a letter to the credit-card company with a copy to the repair shop, explaining the details of the problem and what you want as settlement. Send the letter by certified mail with a return receipt requested. Sometimes the credit-card company or repair shop will attempt to put a "bad mark" on your credit record. You may not be reported as delinquent if you have given the credit-card company notice of your dispute. However, a creditor can report that you are disputing your bill, which can go in your record. The Fair Credit Reporting Act gives you the right to learn what information is in your file and challenge any information you feel is incorrect. You also have the right to have your side of the story added to your file.

Using a credit card will certainly not solve all your auto-repair problems, but it can be a handy ally. For more information about your credit rights, you can write to the Federal Trade Commission, Credit Practices Division, Washington, D.C. 20580.

# The Ten Most Overlooked Maintenance Items

Now that you have a good idea how to get repairs done, we will close this chapter with a list of some very important maintenance items that repair experts often say are overlooked.

1. Change your oil every 7,000 miles. Modern crankcase oil is full of chemicals that can contaminate and deteriorate your engine.
2. Check the brake lines. They have many metal parts and can easily rust.
3. Flush out your radiator every two years.
4. Keep tires fully inflated. You'll improve tire wear, fuel consumption, and vehicle handling.
5. Change the thermostat every two years.
6. Have your disk-brake rotor inspected. It can save you from having to replace the expensive rotor along with the inexpensive pads.
7. Have the front end greased, and the alignment and wheel bearing serviced. Front-end problems are not only expensive to repair but also can be safety hazards.
8. Check the transmission fluid. Change your fluid every 40,000 miles—it will dramatically reduce the incidence of transmission repair.
9. Have your carburetor cleaned and overhauled every 50,000 miles.
10. Be sure the valve lifter is adjusted correctly. It should be checked whenever you hear an unusual tapping noise or every 25,000 miles. If you ignore this adjustment, an expensive valve job is a certainty.

# 7

# Theft Prevention

## Keeping Your Car

A rapidly growing problem for car owners is theft. Car thefts are at an all-time high and will continue to increase as car prices go up and sophisticated car stereos and phones become more common. But there is hope for car owners who realize that the most effective deterrent to car theft or break-in is time.

This section will include a number of simple steps you can take to get time on your side and reduce your chances of having your car stolen. I will also review some more dramatic steps you may want to consider if you live or park in a high-crime area.

Before you invest in an expensive and complicated antitheft device, keep in mind that the market is flooded with expensive devices designed to foil the professional thief. Yet according to the F.B.I most cars are stolen by "amateurs." About eighty percent of the cars stolen are unlocked, and forty percent had the keys in the ignition.

The risk of your car being stolen is an important factor in the cost of your insurance.

## Inexpensive Theft Prevention

Here are some inexpensive ways to protect your car from a thief:

1. Keep your windows tightly rolled up and always lock your car.
2. Never store spare keys in your car.
3. If you keep your car in your driveway, consider facing it toward the street. A thief will be less likely to raise your hood to hot-wire your engine if he or she can be seen from the street.
4. If you regularly park in lots where the attendants take your key, consider getting a different lock for your trunk. Don't tell an attendant how long you'll be unless you have to.
   The basic idea is to make stealing your car time-consuming. If it takes a long time to get into, the thief will most likely give up and try his luck on someone else's car. That means that everything that can be locked is locked.
5. When parking on the street, turn your wheels toward the curb to make it more difficult to push your car away from it.
6. Replace the door-lock buttons with "anti-theft" buttons designed so that a coat hanger or wire cannot grab on. Just the presence of these type of knobs might discourage a thief from even trying.
7. Buy an alarm sticker (even if you don't have an alarm) and put it on one of your windows.
8. Contact your local police department and find out if they have a theft-prevention service. Many departments will provide a sticker and will mark key parts of the car and enter the number into their records. The purpose of these identifying marks is to deter the professional thief who is planning to take the car apart and sell the various compo-

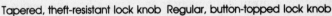

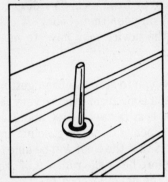 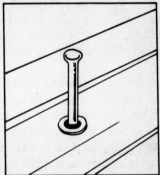

## Lock Knobs

nents. Because the parts can be traced, your car becomes much less attractive.

9. Remove the distributor wire. On the top of the distributor, there is a short wire running to the coil. Removing the wire makes it impossible to start the car. This is a rather inconvenient but effective means of rendering your car inoperable. If you are parking in a particularly suspect place or leaving your car for a long time, you may want to try this. Don't forget to replace it when you want to get going again.

10. Locking gas caps are an inexpensive way to deter vandals from tampering with your fuel supply.

11. If you have a hatchback, consider buying one of the window-shade devices that attaches to the top of the back seat and pulls across the back cargo area, hooking onto the rear opening. This will enable you to hide packages in your cargo area. A cheap way to accomplish the same objective is to carry an old blanket and cover your valuables when you park.

# Specially Installed Anti-theft Devices

Before you invest in an expensive antitheft device, check with your insurance company to see if installing the device will provide you with a discount on your insurance. The discount program (five to fifteen percent on your theft policy) is only available in a few states, and the device may have to meet certain requirements to qualify.

1. A fuel shutoff valve will allow you to stop gas from getting to the engine and will keep someone from driving very far with your car. These devices cost between $100 and $150 to install and will allow you to open or close the gasoline line to the engine. One drawback is that the thief will be able to drive as far as a few blocks before he or she runs out of gas. If your car is missing, check the neighborhood first!

2. Another device to deter the pro is a second ignition switch. In order to start your car, you will have to activate a hidden switch. Time is the thief's worst enemy, and the longer it takes to start your car, the more likely the thief is to give up.

3. The most common antitheft devices on the market are alarms. These can cost up to $300 to $550 installed. The complexity of the systems range from simply setting off your horn when someone opens your door to setting off elaborate sirens when someone merely bumps the car. These alarms are turned off and on by an exterior key-operated switch. This antitheft device may work, but it can be annoying if it goes off at the wrong time. Some people simply have the switch mounted on their car and hope that its presence will intimidate the thief.

4. A relatively simple, but not always effective, antitheft device is called the Krooklok. It is a bar that locks the steering wheel to the brake pedal, making it impossible to steer or to use the brakes. A Krooklok will deter sophisticated amateurs, but the pros can get one off.

# Getting It Back

Here are some tips to help get your car back if it is stolen:

1. Mark your car in several hard-to-find spots on the engine and body. Or drop a business card down the slot between the door and window. If your stolen car is recovered, these things would help identify it.
2. Don't keep your title or registration in the glove compartment unless your state law requires it. That makes it easier for the thief to sell the car.
3. Review your theft-insurance policy. If you don't get your car back, your only recourse will be adequate theft insurance. Is your policy for full coverage, or is there a deductible? Does it cover items stolen from the car or stolen with it? Does it provide for a rental car if your car is stolen?

    Insurance usually covers only the average value of your car when it was stolen. If you feel your car is worth more because of special equipment or unusually good condition, ask for *stated-amount coverage*. The extra cost may be worth it.

# 8
## Resolving Complaints and Problems

## Resolving Your Complaints

It's no surprise that auto-repair complaints regularly top the list of business-complaint statistics—each year we spend billions of dollars on car repairs, and few among us have not been victimized by a repair rip-off. While the statistics are overwhelming, knowing how to handle a repair complaint can tip the odds of resolving these inevitable problems in your favor.

This section is designed to help you resolve complaints, both for brand-new cars under warranty or cars you have owned for a lifetime.

The single most important step you can take to resolving problems in your favor is to keep accurate records. The following items are indispensable for speedy complaint reduction: service invoices, paid bills, letters written to the manufacturer or the owner of the repair facility, and written repair estimates from independent mechanics.

Here are six key steps to resolving general repair problems:

1. Go back to the repair facility that did the work with a written list of the problems. Be sure to keep a copy of the list. The repair shop should have the opportunity to make good on a mistake. When you take the car back, speak directly to the service manager (not the service writer who wrote up your original repair order). Ask the manager to test-drive the car with you so you can point out the problem.

2. The next step is to take the car to a mechanic you trust for an independent examination.

---

*Tip:* In many cities, the AAA offers an independent diagnostic program for both members and nonmembers.

---

Be prepared to pay $30 to $35 for a written statement describing the problem and telling how it may be fixed. Give your repair shop a copy. If your car is under warranty, do not allow any warranty repair by an independent mechanic; you may not be able to receive reimbursement from the manufacturer.

3. If the repair shop does not respond to your independent assessment, present your problem to a complaint-handling panel. If the problem is with a new-car dealer or you feel the manufacturer is responsible, check your owner's manual to see if they have an arbitration program. (See page 115 for more on arbitration.) If the problem is solely with an independent dealer, your local Better Business Bureau may be able to mediate your complaint or offer an arbitration hearing. In any case the BBB should enter your complaint into its files on that particular establishment.

---

*Tip:* When contacting any complaint-handling program, determine how long it takes, who makes the final decision, whether you are bound by that decision, and whether the panel handles all problems or only warranty complaints.

---

4. If there are no mediation panels, contact private consumer groups or local government agencies. A phone call or letter from them may persuade a repair facility to take action. Another suggestion is to call or write to your local "action line" newspaper columnist, newspaper editor, or radio or TV broadcaster. Send a copy of your letter to the repair shop.

5. Unfortunately, the next step is to bring suit against the dealer, manufacturer, or repair facility in small-claims court. The fee for filing an action in such a court is usually small, and you can act as your own attorney, saving attorney's fees. There is a monetary limit, which varies from state to state, on the amount you can claim. Your local consumer-affairs office, state attorney general's office, or the clerk of the court should be able to tell you how to file such a suit.

6. If you don't feel comfortable about going to small-claims court, then select an attorney who has had experience handling automotive problems. If you don't know of one, the lawyer-referral service listed in the telephone directory can provide the names of attorneys who deal with automobile problems. If you can't afford an attorney, contact your Legal Aid society.

If your problem involves getting a factory-authorized dealership to repair your car under warranty, take the following steps:

1. Make sure you have a copy of the warranty available and call the problem to the dealer's attention before the end of the warranty period.

2. After you have given the dealer a reasonable opportunity to fix your car, contact the manufacturer's representative (also called the zone representative) in your area. This person can authorize the dealer to make repairs or take other steps to resolve the dispute. Your dealer will have your zone representative's name and telephone number. Explain the problem and ask for a meeting and a personal inspection of your car.

3. If you can't get satisfaction from the zone representative, call or write the manufacturer's customer-relations department. Your owner's manual contains the phone number and address.

4. If these three steps don't bring action, then present your problem to a complaint-handling panel or the arbitration program in which the manufacturer of your car participates. See the following pages for information.

5. If you complain about a problem during the warranty period, you have a right to have the problem fixed even after the warranty runs out. If your warranty has not been honored, you may be able to "revoke acceptance"—that is, return the car to the dealer. If you are successful, you may be entitled to a replacement car or a full refund of the purchase price and reimbursement of legal fees under the Magnuson-Moss Warranty Act. Or, if you are covered by one of the state lemon laws, you may be able to return the car and receive a refund or replacement from the manufacturer. For more information on lemon laws, see the following pages.

You may also contact the Center for Auto Safety, 2001 S St., NW, Washington, D.C. 20009. This organization can provide the names of lawyers in your area who have handled automobile consumer problems. The Center for Auto Safety also has published *The Lemon Book*, a detailed 236-page guide to resolving automobile complaints. The book is available for $8.60 from the above address.

## Using the Lemon Laws

A lemon is a car that just doesn't work properly. It may have one little problem after another, or just one big problem that never seems to get fixed. It has always been very difficult to obtain a refund if a car turns out to be a lemon. Because it is hard to define exactly what constitutes a lemon, it is difficult to win a case against a manufacturer.

As a result of this problem, most states have passed "lemon

laws," and the rest are considering them. Although each state has a different version of the law, there are some similarities: they establish a period of coverage, usually one year from delivery or the written warranty period, whichever is shorter; they may require some form of noncourt arbitration; and, most important, they define a lemon. In most states a lemon is defined as a new car, truck, or van that has been taken back to the shop at least four times for the same repair or is out of service for a total of thirty days.

If you need to use a lemon law, you must first determine if your state has one. Contact the attorney general in care of your state capitol. If there is a state lemon law, find out how it works.

Some of the consumer groups listed on page 118 are set up specifically to help lemon owners. Contact them for some very helpful advice.

The three keys to successfully using the lemon laws are:

1. Keep good records. All repair attempts and days out of service should be documented. Keep copies of everything. When in doubt, keep it!
2. Provide proper notice. It is very important that you follow the right procedure for notifying the manufacturer of your problem. If written notice to the manufacturer is required, it is best to send a certified, return-receipt-requested letter to the customer-relations office *and* nearest regional office listed in your owner's manual. In the letter, state your car's problem and a very brief history of repair attempts. Make sure you send this notice before the trip to the shop that will qualify your car as a lemon if the repair is unsuccessful.
3. Use arbitration. If the warranty for your car includes an arbitration program, most laws require that you use the program before claiming a refund or replacement. Get the details on the local arbitration programs from your state attorney general. (See the following section for some important tips on arbitration.)

# Arbitration Programs

Arbitration is a relatively new method of resolving automobile-repair problems. In most cases, both parties present their cases to a mediator or arbitration panel that decides on the merits of the complaint. The benefit of arbitration is that it is somewhat informal, relatively speedy, and you do not need a lawyer to present your case. You may seek repairs, reimbursement for expenses, or a refund for or replacement of your car through these programs. Resolving a problem through arbitration is usually faster and less expensive than going to court. You do not have to have a lemon law in your state in order to participate in arbitration programs.

Most manufacturers now have arbitration programs or subscribe to programs set up by the Better Business Bureau or the National Automobile Dealers Association's AUTOCAP program. Look in your owner's manual and warranty for information on programs that cover you.

The arbitration program will attempt to mediate a resolution between you and the manufacturer or dealer; if that doesn't work, your case will be heard at an arbitration hearing.

These hearings vary among the programs. The BBB program allows you to present your case in person to a volunteer arbitrator. Generally, the other programs will decide on your case based on written submissions by you and the manufacturer.

If an arbitration program is incorporated into your warranty, you usually have to use the program before filing a legal claim. However, federal law requires that arbitration programs incorporated in a warranty be nonbinding on the consumer. That means if you're not satisfied with the decision, you can seek other remedies.

Different arbitration programs have different eligibility requirements, so be sure you are eligible for the program you are considering.

## Five Tips for Arbitration

1. Get a written description of how the program works and make sure you understand the details before deciding to go to arbitration. If you have any questions, do not hesitate to contact the local representatives of the program. Remember, the manufacturer or dealer most likely has more experience with this than you do. Make sure the final decision is nonbinding on you. If the decision is binding on you, you give up your right to appeal.

2. If the program does not allow you to appear at the hearing, make sure your written statement is complete and contains all the appropriate receipts and documentation. If you think of something that you want considered after you have sent your material in, send it in and request that the additional information be considered.

3. Well before the actual hearing or panel meeting, ask the program representative to send you copies of all material submitted by the other party. You may want to respond to this information. Contact the manufacturer's zone manager and request copies of any technical service bulletins that apply to your car. Service bulletins may help you prove your car is defective.

4. Submit copies of all material associated with your problem as well as a copy of your warranty. Make sure all your documents are in chronological order, including a brief outline of the events. Even though you may be very angry about the situation, try to present your case in a calm, logical manner.

5. If you are seeking a refund or replacement of your car in accordance with your state lemon law, do not assume that the panel or arbitrator is completely familiar with the law. You should be prepared to make clear how the lemon law and basic fairness entitle you to what you are asking for, especially if you are seeking a refund or replacement of your car. In most programs, you have to reject the decision in order to go to court or pursue other action. Accepting the decision may limit your rights to pursue further action. You will, however, have additional claims if the manufacturer or

dealer does not act according to the decision or if your car breaks down again.

# Car Owner's Resource Center

Getting action on a particular problem or complaint is often simply a matter of knowing whom to call or where to get help. This section contains some important resources that you can use to help resolve problems or get more information about your car.

## Using the Auto Safety Hotline

The National Highway Traffic Safety Administration (NHTSA) operates a toll-free Auto Safety Hotline. The hotline operators can provide information on safety recalls, crash tests, and tire ratings. In addition, hotline operators can refer you to various government auto-safety experts or take your order for numerous free automobile-related publications.

One of the most important roles of the Auto Safety Hotline is to record your automobile-safety complaints.

To get recall information on a particular automobile, you need to tell the hotline operator the make, model, and year of the car, or the type of equipment involved. You will receive any recall information that NHTSA has about that car or item. This information can be very important if you are not sure whether your car has ever been recalled. If you want a printed copy of the recall information, it will be mailed within twenty-four hours at no charge.

Use the hotline to report a safety problem. You will be mailed a questionnaire asking for information the agency's technical staff will need to evaluate the problem. Often this correspondence leads to recall campaigns. After you fill out and return the questionnaire, the following things will happen:

1. A copy will go to NHTSA's safety-defect investigators.
2. A copy will be sent to the manufacturer of the car or equipment, with a request for help in resolving the problem.

117

HOW TO MAKE YOUR CAR LAST ALMOST FOREVER

*3.* You will be notified that your questionnaire has been received.

If you have other car-related problems, the hotline operators can refer you to the appropriate federal, state, and local government agencies. If you need information about federal safety standards and regulations, you will be referred to the appropriate experts.

If you want crash-test information, call the hotline and tell them the make, model, and year of the car you are interested in, and they will send you a crash-test report. If you want information on tires, the hotline will send you a complete list of tire ratings for most of the tires sold in the U.S. (See page 29 for more information on tire ratings.)

You may call the hotline day or night, seven days a week. If you call at a time when no operators are available, you will receive a recorded message asking you to leave your name and address and a description of the information you are seeking. The appropriate materials will be mailed to you. Operators are available from 7:45 AM to 4:15 PM (Eastern time), Monday through Friday. The NHTSA toll-free hotline number is 800–424–9393 (in Washington, D.C., call 366–0123).

## Consumer Groups

The following consumer groups are available to help car owners resolve problems. Don't hesitate to contact these experts for help or advice. There are probably few problems they haven't seen, and you can benefit from their experience. Some of these organizations offer free or low-cost information kits that may provide the exact material you need to resolve your problem speedily.

Aid for Lemon Owners
21711 West Ten Mile Road
Suite 210
Southfield, MI 48075
313-354-1760
*Focus:* Arbitration, reimbursement of repairs, buy-backs

Audi Victims' Network
777 Old Country Road #2
Plainview, NY 11083
*Focus:* Provides assistance to owners of Audis with sudden-
acceleration problems

Auto Protection Association
292 St. Joseph Blvd., W.
Montreal, Quebec H2V 2N7
514-273-1366
*Focus:* General problems

Center for Auto Sports
Suite 410
2001 S Street, NW
Washington, DC 20009
*Focus:* General problems; provides printed material on many
specific problems

Consumer Action
693 Mission Street
San Francisco, CA 94105
415-777-9635
*Focus:* General problems

Genuine Motown Lemon Club
205 East Southern Avenue
Covington, KY 41015
606-431-5393
*Focus:* General problems

LemonAid
6929 Racehorse Ave.
Rockville, MD 20852
301-231-5243
*Focus:* Arbitration

Lemon on Wheels
4044 Connecticut Ave.
Island Park, NY 11558
516-889-4993
*Focus:* Assistance with lemon law arbitration

Motor Voters
Box 3163
Falls Church, VA 22043
703-448-0002
*Focus:* Auto safety and air bags

### Government Agencies

These are the federal agencies that deal with automobile issues. We have provided a brief description of what they do and how to contact them.

National Highway Traffic Safety Administration
400 7th Street, S.W.
Washington, D.C. 20590
202-366-5972

Issues safety and fuel-economy standards for new motor vehicles; investigates safety defects and enforces recall of defective vehicles and equipment. Conducts research and demonstration programs on vehicle safety and fuel economy, driver safety, and automobile inspection and repair; provides grants for state highway safety programs in areas such as police traffic services, driver education and licensing, emergency medical services, pedestrian safety, and alcohol abuse.

Office of Highway Safety
Federal Highway Administration
400 7th Street, S.W.
Washington, D.C. 20590
202-366-1153

Develops standards to ensure that highways are constructed to reduce the occurrence and severity of accidents.

Federal Trade Commission
Pennsylvania Avenue and Sixth Street, N.W.
Washington, D.C. 20580
202-523-3598

Regulates advertising and credit practices, marketing abuses, and professional services, and ensures that products are properly labeled (as in fuel-economy ratings). The commission covers unfair or deceptive trade practices in motor-vehicle sales and repairs, as well as in nonsafety defects.

Environmental Protection Agency
401 M Street, S.W.
Washington, D.C. 20460
202-382-2090

Responsible for the control and abatement of air and toxic-substance pollution. This includes setting and enforcing air emission standards for motor vehicles and measuring the fuel economy in new vehicles (*EPA Gas Mileage Guide*).

Office of Consumer Litigation
Civil Division
U.S. Dept. of Justice
Washington, D.C. 20530
202-724-6789

Enforces the federal law requiring manufacturers to label each new automobile and forbidding removal or alteration of such labels before delivery to the consumer. The label must contain the make, model, vehicle identification number, dealer's name, basic suggested price, cost for all options installed by the manufacturer, and manufacturer's suggested retail price.

## Automobile Manufacturers

You may want to contact one of the automobile companies to register a complaint, get more information about your car (possibly a copy of your owner's manual), or even send a compliment. Here are names and business addresses of the top

121

executives of each of the major automobile companies doing business in the United States. (This information was current at the time the book went to press. Even if changes occur, letters addressed to the president or CEO at these addresses should get through.)

Mr. Joseph Cappy
President
AMC/Renault
27777 Franklin Road
Southfield, MI 48034

Mr. Gunter Kramer
President and Chairman
BMW of North America, Inc.
BMW Plaza
Montvale, NJ 07645

Mr. Lee A. Iacocca
Chairman of the Board
Chrysler Corporation
P.O. Box 1919
Detroit, MI 48288

Mr. Marik Gosia
President
Fiat Auto U.S.A., Inc.
777 Terrace Avenue
Hasbrouck Heights, NJ 07604

Mr. Donald E. Peterson
Chairman of the Board
Ford Motor Company
The American Road
Dearborn, MI 48121

Mr. Roger B. Smith
Chairman of the Board
General Motors Corporation
General Motors Building
Detroit, MI 48202

Mr. T. Chino
President
American Honda Motor Company, Inc.
100 West Alondra Blvd.
Gardena, CA 90247

Mr. Max Jamiesson
Executive Vice President
Hyundai Motor America
7373 Hunt Avenue
Garden Grove, CA 92642

Mr. Yukio Itagaki
President
American Isuzu Motors, Inc.
2300 Pellissier Place
Whittier, CA 90601

Mr. Graham W. Whitehead
President
Jaguar Cars, Inc.
600 Willow Tree Road
Leonia, NJ 07605

Mr. Hisao Kaide
President
Mazda Motors of America, Inc.
1444 McGraw Avenue
Irvine, CA 92714

Mr. Hans-Jurgen Hinrichs
Chairman of the Board
Mercedes-Benz North America, Inc.
1 Mercedes Benz Drive
Montvale, NJ 07645

Mr. Isao Nishina
Chairman of the Board
Mitsubishi of America, Inc.
10540 Talbert Street
Fountain Valley, CA 92708

Mr. Kazutoshi Hagiwara
President
Nissan (Datsun) Motor Corporation
18501 Figueroa Street
Carson, CA 90248

Mr. Pierre Lemaire
President
Peugeot Motors of America, Inc.
1 Peugeot Plaza
Lyndhurst, NJ 07071

Mr. Peter W. Schutz
Chairman of the Board
Porsche Cars North America
200 S. Virginia Street
Reno, Nevada 89501

Mr. P. Henry Mueller
Chairman of the Board
Saab-Scania of America, Inc.
Saab Drive, P.O. Box 697
Orange, CT 06477

Mr. Harvey Lamm
President
Subaru of America, Inc.
7040 Central Highway
Pennsauken, NJ 08109

Mr. Yukiyasu Togo
President
Toyota Motors Sales-USA, Inc.
19001 S. Western Avenue
Torrance, CA 90509

Mr. Carl H. Hahn
Chairman of the Board
Volkswagen/Audi
888 West Big Beaver Road
Troy, MI 48099

Mr. Peter Gyllenhammar
Chairman of the Board
Volvo of America Corporation
1 Volvo Drive
Rockleigh, NJ 07647

Mr. Malcolm Bricklin
Chairman of the Board
Yugo America, Inc.
645 Fifth Avenue
Suite 712
New York, NY 10022

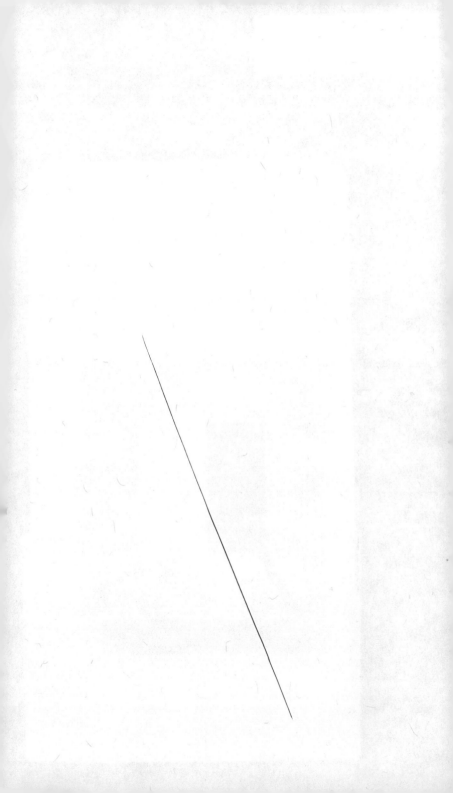